YORK HANDBOO

GENERAL EDITOR:
Professor A.N. Jeffares
(*University of Stirling*)

THE
METAPHYSICAL
POETS

Trevor James
BA BD PH D (LONDON)
Senior Lecturer in English,
Darwin Institute of Technology

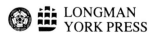

LONGMAN
YORK PRESS

For my parents

YORK PRESS
Immeuble Esseily, Place Riad Solh, Beirut.

LONGMAN GROUP UK LIMITED
Longman House,
Burnt Mill,
Harlow,
Essex

First published 1988

ISBN 0-582-96603-5

Produced by Longman Group (FE) Ltd
Printed in Hong Kong

Contents

Preface

The reputation of the Metaphysical poets and the state of seventeenth-century studies have made great advances in the last fifty years. Whereas at the turn of the century John Donne was a minor name in the *Oxford Book of English Verse* and represented by a mere seven poems, two of which he had not in fact written, the situation is now quite different. The availability both of excellent critical editions of these poets' works and an abundance of specialist literary scholarship testify to the vast improvement in knowledge that we now possess of the literature and culture of the period. Now, and especially since the nineteen-fifties, Donne's reputation and that of the other Metaphysical poets has never been higher. Perhaps even more remarkable, and in contrast to the secular nature of contemporary life, the quality of their religious verse—as literature—is widely appreciated.

Any author of a brief study of this nature will draw upon the results of the labours of others, and I am very conscious of my indebtedness to the research of numerous scholars. In the brief compass of this work I have not favoured any particular line of critical approach but aimed at providing an introduction to the subject. From this I hope that the reader will be encouraged to advance to more detailed and specialised areas of study, where, as Donne remarks in his 'A Valediction: of the Book':

> Here Love's Divines, (since all Divinity
> Is love or wonder) may find all they seek

Trevor James
Darwin 1986

Chapter 1

The wider
context

A label of convenience

BOSWELL: 'Then, Sir, what is poetry?'
JOHNSON: 'Why, Sir, it is much easier to say what it is not. We all *know* what light is; but it is not easy to *tell* what it is.'*

This witty evasion of Boswell's question by Dr Johnson (1709–84) parallels the difficulties experienced when we attempt to define Metaphysical poetry. In fact our predicament is worse; do we even know what we mean? The primary use of the term 'metaphysical' is in philosophy, and the term can be applied to those poems which attempt to express some comprehensive view of the world, such as the *De Natura Rerum* of Lucretius (*c*.99-55BC); the *Divina Commedia* (1472) of Dante (*c*.1265–1321), perhaps too John Milton's (1608–74) *Paradise Lost* (1667). Such poems, observed Sir Herbert Grierson in his influential anthology of the Metaphysical poets (1921), have been 'inspired by a philosophical conception of the universe and the role assigned to the human spirit in the great drama of existence'.† It is a source of confusion to many readers that this philosophical use of 'metaphysical' does not apply to those poets we call the 'Metaphysicals'.

In short, our common literary usage 'Metaphysical poetry' is a specialised term with a specific meaning: it refers to the poetry of John Donne (1571/2–1631) and the 'school' of writers who either copied his style or were at least indebted to his influence during the early seventeenth century. It appears to have originated as literary slang, not to define the content, but to describe a distinctive poetic style and manner. The origins of the term are confused: initially it appears to have been derogatory. An undated letter of Drummond of Hawthornden (1585–1649) refers to poets who make use of 'Metaphysical *Ideas* and *Scholastical Quiddities*'. Here Drummond alludes to a style which is supposedly riddled with the philosophical and theological teachings

* James Boswell, *Life of Johnson*, ed. R.W. Chapman (The World's Classics edition), Oxford University Press, Oxford, 1980, p.744.
† H.J.C. Grierson, *Metaphysical Lyrics and Poems of the Seventeenth Century*, Oxford University Press, Oxford, 1921 (1972), p.xiii.

of the 'Schoolmen', the scholars during the period 1100–1500—such as Abelard (1079–1142), Albertus Magnus (1193–1280), Duns Scotus (?1265–?1308), Ockham (?–?1349), and Peter Lombard (c.1100–c.1160)—who attempted to reconcile the claims of reason with those of religious faith, and whose highly refined methods of disputation on occasion degenerated into irrelevant displays of logic. In Drummond's opinion, the effect of this Scholastic philosophy on poetry was to make it abstract and unduly difficult. This uncomplimentary view was shared by John Dryden (1631–1700) who, in 1693, criticised what he regarded as Donne's excessive use of philosophy. In his dedication to *A Discourse concerning the Original and Progress of Satire*, Dryden tells the Earl of Dorset that Donne 'perplexes the minds of the fair sex with nice [over-subtle] speculations of philosophy, when he should engage their hearts and entertain them with the softnesses of love'.

The use of 'metaphysical' in a descriptive sense appears to have originated in a remark by Samuel Johnson (1709–84) in his *Life of Cowley* (1779): 'About the beginning of the seventeenth century appeared a race of writers that may be termed the metaphysical poets . . . [they] . . . were men of learning, and to show their learning was their whole endeavour.'* Johnson's observation set a critical direction. He identified both the peculiarity of the style he was describing and the philosophical context of the word he had chosen, but he also noted two other crucial features of the early Metaphysical style: its metrical harshness and the sheer variety of its wit.

It is unfortunate that the casual coinage 'Metaphysical' has stuck for it gives the impression that there existed a distinctive and coherent identity between various poets, an impression that is not borne out by closer examination. In short, the arbitrary distinction between a 'Metaphysical' school—which includes John Donne (1571/2–1631), George Herbert (1593–1633), Henry Vaughan (1622–95), Andrew Marvell (1621–78), Thomas Traherne (1637–74) and Richard Crashaw (?1612–49)—and a 'classical' school headed by Ben Jonson (1572–1637) and comprising his so-called 'sons', in particular Robert Herrick (1591–1674), Thomas Carew (?1598–1639), Richard Lovelace (1618–58) and Sir John Suckling (1609–42)—however useful it is in some respects, has proved misleading. In 1921 T.S. Eliot (1888–1965) remarked, 'Not only is it extremely difficult to define metaphysical poetry, but difficult to decide what poets practise it and in which of their verses . . . It is difficult to find any precise use of metaphor, simile, or other conceit, which is common to all the poets and at the same time important enough as an element of style to isolate these poets as a group.'†

* James Boswell, *Life of Johnson*, p.677.
† T.S. Eliot, 'The Metaphysical Poets', in *Selected Prose*, ed. J. Hayward, Peregrine/Penguin, Harmondsworth, 1963, p.105.

A 'warlike and tragical age'

History

Since the literature of any period cannot be separated from the events of its time and the contemporary forces that influenced the writers, a brief summary of events and ideas in the seventeenth century is necessary as a context for the Metaphysicals.

The span of the English Renaissance is usually taken to be from about 1509 to 1660. An age when individual life could be short, violent and brutish, it endured two major armed confrontations. The first concerned the European rivalries between Catholic Europe and Protestant England in the mid-sixteenth century, and reached its most critical and embittered stage when English suspicion of Spain and Rome reached a climax in the defeat of the Spanish Armada (1588). Strengthened by the flight of Protestant refugees from persecution in Catholic Europe, this suspicion continued through the early seventeenth century and was exacerbated by the English Jesuits and the Catholic recusants—those who remained Roman Catholics after the English Reformation—whose numbers in 1603 have been estimated at about 40,000. The Gunpowder Plot belongs to this period of tension, and the various events associated with it dramatically demonstrate the fears and prejudices of the time.

The English Revolution and Civil War towards the middle of the seventeenth century was the second major disturbance, and the most influential as far as most of the Metaphysical poets—except Donne and Herbert—were concerned. The troubles of the Civil War stemmed from the follies of the Stuart kings. James I (1566–1625) was politically inept, and Charles I (1600–49) no better: both failed to grasp the changing political and social reality of their realm, in particular the growing power of Parliament. The consequence was a clash between Crown and Parliament in which a small ruling class fought within its own ranks for power. From 1629 until 1640 Charles ruled without Parliament, but finally convened it to raise funds. This 'Short Parliament' was dissolved after three weeks in 1640 and a few months later was succeeded by the 'Long Parliament' which, in 1641, drafted a 'Grand Remonstrance' against the King. Civil war began in 1642 after the King entered Parliament with his troops to arrest five MPs. After four years of civil war Charles was defeated and was executed in 1649. Under Oliver Cromwell (1599–1658) there emerged a parliamentary government which split into two factions, Independent and Presbyterian. Cromwell took sole charge of the nation in 1653 when he established a Commonwealth and was named 'Lord Protector'. The Commonwealth formally ended two years after Cromwell's death when Charles II (1630–85) landed at Dover in May 1660.

Society

The social context of the seventeenth century was marked by change as
wealth shifted in English society. Economic factors were crucial. Infla-
tion had wrecked the fortunes of some ancient families, while traditional social relationships had been destabilised by an agrarian revolution as enclosures of common lands and raised rents drove rural labourers to the towns; and the traditional yeomen of England resented
the high prices caused by monopolies and the efforts of Archbishop
Laud (1573–1645) to increase tithe payments. As a new economic
order arose dependent on trade, industry and modern farming techniques, so economic power passed from the House of Lords to the House
of Commons, and the Commons increasingly asserted their strength
against Lords, Church and Crown. The peerage, which numbered at
most one hundred and twenty lords, had been weakened as estates and
titles changed hands, and the landed aristocracy no longer saw its fortunes tied to the monarchy. Under the Tudor monarchs the sale of titles
and creation of new orders had made traditional supporters of the
crown disaffected and created a new type of aristocracy with little taste
for traditional responsibilities. On the other hand, the Church,
through its twenty-six bishops, clung to its powers and sought to realise
them through the Crown—and thereby helped its downfall. More
important were members of the squirearchy. They dominated the
House of Commons and defended the rights of a landed gentry. In the
absence of a standing army, these men, together with the peerage,
maintained the law in return for social and economic privileges. It is
important to note that while the leaders of the 'Long Parliament'
limited the power of the monarch and revealed a new notion of authority, they also had a vested interest in a stable realm. Peers such as
Warwick, Essex, Manchester, were men of wealth and substance, not
radical malcontents.

Court and city life were centred upon London, which, as the focus
for fashionable and intellectual life, forced potential factions together.
The Court generally represented a European perspective, and its art
and music echoed the tastes of Catholic Europe which the classical
'paganism' of Jonson and Herrick, and the Baroque sensibility of the
Metaphysicals, generally reflected. This was in stark contrast to the
Puritans' outlook, many of whom were scandalised by the masques of
the Court, its corruptions, and what were felt to be its pro-Catholic
tendencies. London, then, provided a focus for opposition to the Monarchy. In London the Presbyterians were in the majority—and this was
unique in England. Furthermore, there was the urban mob: a new political and social factor. It was made up of men driven by pressures
beyond their control, no longer governed by notions of traditional

social order, their numbers augmented by disaffected rural labourers, graduates and students from the Inns of Court. This mob was something which could be quickly raised to besiege Parliament and provide the basis for political opposition.

The Inns of Court—London's Bohemia

London's Inns of Court—the Middle Temple, Inner Temple, Gray's Inn and Lincoln's Inn—were centres for the intellectual life of London at the turn of the century. The students and fellows of these London law schools often came direct from Oxford and Cambridge to read law after having completed their studies in classics and rhetoric and before undertaking positions in government service. The largest educated community in London, these students added a cultivated bohemian flavour to the city's intellectual life, and provided enthusiastic support for the theatre and literary fashions that emerged. Their tastes were reflected in the verse satires of Hall (1574–1656), Marston (?1575–1634) and Davies (?1565–1618), who drew upon the example of the Roman satirist Juvenal (c.AD60–130) for their denunciation of contemporary society and its vices, and were also reflected in the dramatic satiric character of the malcontent who appeared in the dramas of Middleton (1570–1627) and Webster (?1580–1625). From this stimulating milieu issued the ironic, learned, concentrated wit we associate with the Metaphysicals.

An attitude to experience

If literature is to have any bearing on society it is probably inevitable, even necessary, that a critic should judge it against his pulse; value it in the light of the deepest concerns of his own age. By the same token, we may value Donne—or indeed any of the Metaphysicals—because of their *difference* from us, because they demonstrate a way of thinking and speaking no longer possible for us; or in other words because the variety and energy of the Metaphysical style are sustained by an intellectual and spiritual coherence that has since been eroded from our world.

A unified sensibility

The theory which views the seventeenth century as a period in which the Civil War marked a 'dissociation of sensibility' stems from T.S. Eliot's influential criticism. He portrays a pre-Civil War society as materially and spiritually coherent while still diverse: in short a society which possessed a 'unified sensibility' that 'could devour any kind of experience'.* After the Civil War this unity had been shattered, or, as he expresses it, 'a dissociation of sensibility set in, from which we have never recovered.'† Contentious though the theory is, it has provided a stimulating approach to the literature of the post-Civil War period. The fact is that in a poet such as Donne we are impressed by his capacity to give coherence to diversity, and fashion from the tensions of flesh and spirit, mind and feeling, a consciousness in which a thought has emotional fullness and in which flesh expresses spirit. In T.S. Eliot's often quoted words: 'a thought to Donne was an experience'.‡ 'The Ecstasy' is eloquent demonstration of this:

As our blood labours to beget
  Spirits, as like souls as it can,
Because such fingers need to knit
  That subtle knot, which makes us man:

So must pure lovers' souls descend
  T' affections, and to faculties,
Which sense may reach and apprehend,
  Else a great prince in prison lies.

An introspective sensibility

Donne's style reflects a highly individual, introspective and intellectual consciousness. In fact for all Metaphysical poetry it is generally true (with some notable exceptions, such as the political poems of Marvell) that it is private rather than public poetry. This marks an outlook characteristic of the Renaissance. One passage from the Italian political theorist Machiavelli (1469–1527), shows this attitude very clearly:

At nightfall I return home and seek my writing room, and, divesting myself on its threshold of my rustic garments, stained with mud and mire, I assume courtly attire, and thus suitably clothed, enter within the ancient courts of ancient men, by whom, being cordially welcomed, I am fed with the food that alone is mine, and for which I was born, and am not ashamed to hold discourse with them, and inquire the motives of their actions; and these men in their humanity reply to me, and for the space of four hours I feel no weariness, remember no trouble, no longer fear poverty, no longer dread death; my whole being is absorbed in them.**

* T.S. Eliot, 'The Metaphysical Poets', p.111.
† T.S. Eliot, 'The Metaphysical Poets', p.111.
‡ T.S. Eliot, 'The Metaphysical Poets', p.110.
** Quoted in D. Bush, *Prefaces to Renaissance Literature*, Harvard University Press, Cambridge, Massachusetts, 1965, p.12.

The solitary figure of the philosopher in his book-lined room recurs throughout the Renaissance, and here Machiavelli perfectly expresses this Renaissance individualism, its openness to knowledge and experience. Indeed so does Montaigne (1533–92) whose influence in English thought, with his moral relativism and general scepticism, certainly dates from the translation of his *Essays* into English by John Florio (*c.*1533–1625). One of Montaigne's most quoted contributions to Western thought has been the phrase 'the human condition'. It is worth comparing Machiavelli's comments with the attitude set out in Montaigne's famous meditation *Of Solitude*. This passage vividly expresses Renaissance introspection:

A man that is able may have wives, children, goods, and chiefly health, but not so tie himself unto them that his felicity depend on them. We should reserve a storehouse for ourselves, what need soever chance, altogether ours and wholly free, wherein we may hoard up and establish true liberty and principal retreat and solitariness, wherein we must go alone to ourselves to take our ordinary entertainment, and so privately that no acquaintance or communication of any strange thing may therein find place; there to discourse, to meditate and laugh, as without wife, without children and goods, without train or servants, that if by any occasion they be lost it seem not strange to us to pass it over. We have a mind moving and turning in itself; it may keep itself company; it hath wherewith to offend and defend, wherewith to receive and wherewith to give . . .

A speculative approach to life, which absorbed old and new, carried over into most disciplines but also marked something of a spiritual crisis in which old values were challenged. For many, history and literature still retained their old moral significance: where the former was believed to be moral instruction by example, the latter was similarly expected to incite and encourage virtuous life and action. But intellectual and spiritual certainties had been shaken along with the political and social order. The seventeenth-century developments of the English Renaissance are marked by a greater perturbation of spirit, the darkening of vision displayed in Shakespeare's later tragedies. Donne's detachment, his questioning intellect, mark a pervasive attitude where everything is tested, debated and considered from a variety of positions so that its essential 'truth' may be known. Just as Gloucester remarks in *King Lear* 'We have seen the best of our time', so Donne observes in 'An Anatomy of the World' that 'Our age was iron and rusty too'.

The cultural and intellectual context

A different world picture

In some ways poets in the early seventeenth century were especially fortunate. It was still possible to view the world in the ordered hierarchical
manner that the Elizabethans inherited from the Middle Ages. Empiri-
cal philosophy had not yet fully emerged, and the notional philosophy
of the Schoolmen still had currency. Contemporary works, such as Sir
Thomas Browne's (1605–82) *Religio Medici* (1642), demonstrate the
eclecticism of Renaissance sensibility: the assumptions, references and
intellectual correspondences which could be made and which were
recorded with relish. Both the universe and man, it was believed, could
be divided into two portions: one subject to change, the other eternal.
In theological terms this division corresponded to an order of Nature
and an order of Grace. Man was a 'little world', a microcosm of the
greater: his body was subject to nature, to mutability, but the soul was
eternal and the object of divine grace. In the world, divided into
spheres, those spheres below the sphere of the moon were subject to
change, those above were immutable. As elaborated from the ancient
philosophers, Aristotle (384–322BC) and Ptolemy (*c.*AD90–168), the
system was orderly and subtle with a scale of being rising from inani-
mate nature to the Godhead. Poems such as Donne's 'Twickenham
Garden' or 'A Nocturnal Upon St Lucy's Day' demonstrate this, while
Sir Thomas Browne's *Religio Medici* elaborates on the unique place of
man in such a system:

> We are onely that amphibious piece between a corporal and spiritual
> Essence, that middle form that links those two together, and makes
> good the method of God and Nature, that jumps not from extreams,
> but unites the incompatible distances by some middle and participat-
> ing natures. That we are the breath and similitude of God, it is indis-
> putable, and upon record of Holy Scripture; but to call ourselves a
> Microcosm, or little World, I thought it only a pleasant trope of
> rhetorick, till my neer judgement and second thoughts told me there
> was a real truth therein. (section xxxiii)

Such a coherent view of the world generated ways of thinking and
expression which helped to cement the social fabric. On a broad social
level touching nearly every sector of society were the great 'commonplaces' or ideas which spanned the centuries. Biblical and classical texts
were particularly influential, indeed the sermons and homilies of the
Church marked a continuity of style which went back to the Middle
Ages, but there were others: the *theatrum mundi* (the 'theatre of the
world') or the *locus amoenus*, the 'lovely place', with the expectations

of, and interest in, an ideal spot of which Eden was the archetype and which the pastoral genre and seventeenth-century theories of landscape gardening recalled.

A continuity of ideas

Beyond the apparently 'unified sensibility' of the Metaphysical poets is the complexity of Renaissance humanism. For England, isolated from the Italian Renaissance—the *quattrocento*—by its northernness and its insularity, the Renaissance came much later than on the Continent. While English writers were open to the influence of new learning upon established habits of thought, they were still close to the intellectual order of the medieval world. Despite the revolutionary impact of Copernicus (1473–1543) on views of the astronomical system in 1543 and the work of Vesalius (1514–64) on theories about the human body, beliefs in a geocentric universe, astrological medicine and other such traditional doctrines continued until well into the seventeenth century. The impact of 'new' knowledge is obvious in such poems as Donne's first *Anniversary*, 'An Anatomy of the World':

And new philosophy calls all in doubt,
The element of fire is quite put out;
The sun is lost, and th' earth, and no man's wit
Can well direct him where to look for it.

In Donne's case the mix of medieval and new learning is particularly clear. His interest in astronomers such as Bruno (?1548–?99), Kepler (1571–1630), Galileo (1564–1642) and Copernicus, and the possible implications of their ideas is amply demonstrated in his writing. Similarly we know that he was familiar with Renaissance humanists such as Montaigne. On the other hand, the medieval aspect was equally important to Donne: he knew the scholastic philosophers, the forms of 'knowledge' and disputation in scholastic thought, and frequently referred to St Thomas Aquinas (1224–74). The same can be said for his allusions to law, philosophy and theology. He demonstrates that Renaissance writers in general—not just the Metaphysical school—inherited medieval traditions as much as they foreshadowed the modern and scientific world.

In short, while the old humanism had not been abandoned, its reassuring semblance of coherence had flagged amidst much speculation and discussion of possibility. A variety of sources can demonstrate this. Long before Donne, Gabriel Harvey (1545–1630) had remarked that there abounded 'every day, fresh-spun new opinions: heresy in divinity, in philosophy, in humanity, in manners, grounded upon much hearsay; doctors contemned: the text known of most, understood

of few, magnified of all, practised of none'.* Drummond of Hawthornden had echoed Donne in 1623 when he said:

> The element of fire is quite put out, the air is but water rarified, the
> earth is found to move and is no more the centre of the universe, is
> turned into a magnet; stars are not fixed, but swim in the ethereal
> space, comets are mounted above the planets; some affirm that there
> is another world of men and sensitive creatures ... in the moon; the
> sun is lost ... Thus sciences, by the diverse motions of this globe of
> the brain of man, are become opinions, nay errors, and leave the
> imagination in a thousand labyrinths. What is all we know with
> what we know not?†

A poet in the Spenserian tradition such as Drayton (1563−1631) also
echoes this radical uncertainty:

> Certainly there's scarce one found that now
> Knows what t'approve, or what to disallow;
> All arsey-varsey, nothing is its own,
> But to our proverb, all turned upside down ...
> Where hell is heaven, and heaven is now turned hell.‡

The Renaissance humanist's classical and Christian background

The foundations of the images, elaborate allusions and conceits of the
Metaphysical writers are the cultural assumptions of the English Renaissance. Behind all the writing of this period is a comprehensive
humanistic tradition, nurtured by a classical and Christian education,
which enabled writers to assume that their audience was familiar with
classical literature, and possessed of a common stock of knowledge
and outlook.

The origins of Renaissance humanism are complex, but they can be
roughly dated from Petrarch's (1304–74) repudiation of medieval for
classical Latin, and of scholastic dispute for the arts of rhetoric in the
mid-fourteenth century. The term 'humanist' is an anglicisation of the
Italian 'umanista'—a Latin teacher. It can be traced back to Cicero
(106–43BC), whose 'humanitas' means both humanity and the cultural
education which develops it—hence our 'Humanities'. In short a
humanist was a classical scholar who imitated the language and style of

---

* Quoted in H. Hadyn, *The Counter-Renaissance*, New York, 1950, p.13; and in C.
Hill, *Intellectual Origins of the English Revolution*, Clarendon Press, Oxford, 1965, p.8.
† W. Drummond, 'A Cypresse Grove', in *Poetical Works*, ed. L. and E. Kastner, 1913,
vol. ii. p.78; quoted in C. Hill, *Intellectual Origins of the English Revolution*.
‡ M. Drayton, 'To My Noble Friend Master William Browne, of the evil time', in
Works, ed. J.W. Hebel, Vol III, pp.209-11. Quoted in C. Hill, *Intellectual Origins of
the English Revolution*.

classical literature, and pursued its classical values. This connection from the beginning between Renaissance humanism and education continued into the later English Renaissance through such writers as Roger Ascham (1515–68) in his *The Scholemaster* (1570) and John Milton in his *Tractate of Education* (1644). The invention of printing (*c.*1450) fed the pragmatic scholarship of the Renaissance and its affirmation of classical literature and culture. Through such international scholars as Erasmus (?1466–1536) these values were brought to England and developed, especially by John Colet (1466-1519) and Sir Thomas More (1478–1535).

A profile of the seventeenth-century man of letters suggests the cultural milieu. He was a classical scholar: Latin was the foundation of his education and he was well read in its poetry, history and philosophy; he might also have had some knowledge of Greek, though he would have encountered most of its literature through Latin and English translations. In poetry, the *Iliad* of Homer (700 or 800BC), Virgil's (70–19BC) *Aeneid* and Ovid's (43BC–8AD) *Metamorphoses*; in philosophy, Plato's (*c.*427–348BC) *Symposium* and *Republic*, as well as Aristotle's *Nicomachean Ethics* and Cicero's *Of Duties* were all familiar.

The seventeenth-century writer also synthesised Christian and classical traditions: that is to say, he read classical literature in the light of his Christian beliefs and the two world views with their often conflicting outlooks coexisted. Significantly, the Renaissance saw the rediscovery of classical texts through major translations from Latin to English, such as Arthur Golding's (?1536 – ?1605) translation of Ovid in 1567, and George Chapman's (?1559–?1634) Homer—the *Iliad* in 1611 and the *Odyssey* in 1616. The consequences were crucial: Ovid was transformed from a philosophical and religious poet to being appreciated as a major poet of erotic verse.

Since most humanists attempted to harmonise classical values with a practical Christianity (especially Erasmus who applied to Scripture the critical textual and philological methods that Italian humanists had applied to classical literature), we can also assume such writers to have been Christians, with a good working knowledge of the Bible and the liturgy. The humanist would be aware of the essentials of the major works of religious controversy, both in his own century and those of the early Church Fathers, particularly, for example, Augustine's *City of God*. His knowledge of the classical and Christian traditions came through both a first-hand reading of the texts—the Bible, the Fathers of the Church, the Latin and Greek texts—and through careful reading of those second-hand sources, popular handbooks and encyclopedias which digested the primary materials for him.

The principles of humanism reflect a consistent practical application. At least three should be noted: (1) the imitation of the classical writers in style and moral content; (2) the pragmatic application of learning to improve life; (3) a sense of duty which is reflected in the Renaissance fascination with variations of Plato's philosopher-king described in his *The Republic*, V-VII. English humanists, largely as a consequence of Erasmus's efforts, sought to realise something of the Platonic model by their orientation toward court and public life. Numerous works were written which endeavoured to instruct rulers and those in public life on how to exercise their responsibilities: these include *The Boke named the Governour* (1531) by Sir Thomas Elyot (1499–1546) and *Utopia* (1516) by Sir Thomas More. The tension between wisdom and its application was a profound one, often with drastic consequences, as the death of Sir Thomas More demonstrated. Hence the recurring theme in the literature—Herbert, Marvell and Milton are obvious examples—of the choice between leisure (*otium*) and business (*negotium*), the pleasures of the garden as a place for contemplation, against the duties of the court where actions may be influenced.

Religious life

Religious thought was a catalyst, all the more influential for literature since many of the poets—including Giles Fletcher the younger (?1588–1623), Southwell (?1561–95), Donne, Crashaw and Herbert—were ordained. The numerous shifts in religious allegiance mirror the centrality of, and the stress occasioned by, religious faith in the seventeenth century: Donne moved from Catholicism to Anglicanism; Crashaw from Anglicanism to Catholicism; Milton from Anglicanism, through Presbyterianism to Separatism. It is impossible to understand the literature of the Renaissance without some knowledge of the religious context against which these writers worked.

Particular events symbolise the character of the period, the extent to which it was a time of social flux and even occasional ideological radicalism. The execution of Charles I and the earlier publication in the 1560s of the Geneva Bible with its highly political marginal notes are such events. Ideas, in particular religious ideas, were considered vital and potent. In the words of the historian Christopher Hill:

> Religion was the idiom in which the men of the seventeenth century thought. One does not need to accept the idiom, or to take it at its face value, to see that it cannot be ignored or rejected as a simple reflex of economic needs. Any adequate interpretation of the English Revolution must give full place to questions of religion and Church Government, must help us to grasp the political and social implications of theological heresy.*

* C. Hill, *Puritanism and Revolution*, Mercury Books, London; reprinted by Heinemann, London, 1965, p.29.

Use of the Bible as a handbook for such radicalism as that of John Milton, the Leveller John Lilburne (?1614–57) and Oliver Cromwell, symbolised a widespread interest in forms of millenialism: how to make a new man, a new society, a new world. The most specific manifestation of this was demonstrated in 1649. Hedged as royalty was by sanctity, the shock of Charles I's execution was immense: on hearing the news 'women miscarried, men fell into melancholy, some with consternations expired'.*

The intellectual upheaval

The history of the period and the development of its literature intimately reflect profound religious concerns brought about by the radically expanded intellectual horizons of the Renaissance humanists. All the new knowledge had an impact upon established religious authority, and in its turn produced a deep unease. In physical science the discoveries of Copernicus, Kepler, Galileo and Francis Bacon (1561 – 1626) had demonstrated a belief that observed physical phenomena should serve as the basis for conclusions about the world. The philosophical consequences of this can be seen, on the one hand, in the thought of Thomas Hobbes (1588–1679) who attacked scholastic philosophy and based his approach upon the natural sciences, and John Locke (1632–1704), the founder of English empiricism; and, on the other hand, in the work of Descartes (1596–1650), who, though a devout Roman Catholic, methodically doubted everything, and sought to argue for the existence of God from his famous premise—*Cogito, ergo sum*, 'I think, therefore I am'. What may seem remarkable now is that none of these scientists or philosophers denied the superior authority of religion. Indeed few writers in the period ever denied the existence of a personal God, though they questioned the specific teachings of theology.

Protestant and Catholic

Both the Protestant and Catholic Reformations marked a common impulse: both sought to bring the Church back to a Christian ideal, but differed as to how this was to be accomplished. In the seventeenth century both Catholic and Protestant reformers had to come to terms with the new learning, even while disputes continued as to doctrine and government. Hugo Grotius (1583–1645), the Dutch jurist who had been an ambassador in London in 1613, published *De Veritate*

* W. Sanderson, *A Complete History of the Life and Raigne of King Charles* (1658). Quoted in C. Hill, *Intellectual Origins of the English Revolution*, Clarendon Press, Oxford, 1965, p.5.

Religionis Christianae (1627) in which he argued that the views of all Christianity could be reconciled on a common basis of piety and scriptural evidence. The great success of this work reflected a widespread exasperation with ecclesiastical conflict, and the sense that there were more fundamental issues to be engaged.

Protestantism: Anglican and Puritan

The name Protestant was attached initially to the followers of Luther (*c.*1483–1546), Zwingli (1484–1531) and, later, Calvin (1509–64). English Protestantism developed from the European Reformation of the sixteenth century which was encouraged by the critical weapons humanism provided, and, by the seventeenth century, in England 'Protestant' meant 'orthodox Protestant', that is, it excluded such sects as the Baptists and Quakers which were opposed to the prevailing views on Church organisation. The variety of religious opinion in England during the seventeenth century was remarkable: the Baptists repudiated infant baptism, and insisted upon a 'gathered' church composed solely of 'Believers'; the Quakers rejected war and swearing oaths; the Fifth Monarchy Men advocated the creation of a new society through armed rebellion. All these sectarian influences were founded upon religious convictions which brought them into conflict with established authority, created an environment which approximated the religious anarchy of Reformation Europe, and created the basis for some of the extremes endured during the Commonwealth.

In England the Reformation was carried out under the instigation of Henry VIII (1509–47) who essentially tried to maintain the structure of Catholicism without the Pope. A national Protestant church took shape under the Archbishop of Canterbury, Thomas Cranmer (1489–1556), with his Book of Common Prayer (1549/1552). The sacraments, vestments, liturgy and episcopal government of Catholicism were retained in the Church of England and remained a source of contention with the Puritans—those who thought that a more thorough 'reformation' of the Church should be carried out. Only under Elizabeth I (1558–1603) was the Church recognised to be 'reformed' and Protestant, the most eloquent statement of its position being that by Richard Hooker (?1554–1600) in his superb *Laws of Ecclesiastical Polity* (1594).

The most distinctive feature of Protestantism, English and European, is that it sought to reform the Church by breaking away from Roman Catholicism, and, in place of Papal authority, appealed to the authority of the Bible and the teachings of the early Church. One telling instance of this is the bold affirmation of the scholar William Chilingworth (1602–44) in his *The Religion of Protestants. A Safe Way to Salvation* (1637):

I do not understand the Doctrine of Luther, or Calvin, or Melancthon, nor the Confession of Augusta, or Geneva, nor the Catechism of Heidelberg, nor the Articles of the Church of England, no nor the harmony of the Protestant Confessions, but that wherein they all agree, and which they all subscribe with a greater harmony, as a perfect rule of their faith and actions; that is, the BIBLE.*

The Puritan reformers were a vital factor in seventeenth-century life. In the seventeenth century 'Puritan' had no precise meaning. It generally indicated an attitude towards Church reform and religious life which could be found in devout Anglicans, Calvinists and Sectarians. From these reformers there was constant pressure for further reform of Church ritual, policy and discipline. As a consequence Anglicanism was violently torn between Lutheran and Calvinistic or Puritan factions. Perhaps the most telling instance is the occasion when the Puritans met James I on his way from Scotland to London in April 1603, and presented him with the 'Millenary Petition' with its stock objections to the Book of Common Prayer, the use of the sign of the cross at baptism, the ring in matrimony, the use in Church of lessons from the Old Testament's Apocrypha, and the wearing of the surplice by the clergy.

James I rebuffed the Puritans' demands and the basis for a later crisis was established. When Archbishop Laud instituted a rigorous policy of maintaining Anglican teaching and discipline, conflict became virtually inevitable. Under Charles I, Laud ensured that Puritan clergy were deprived of their livings for refusing to wear the surplice, kneel at Communion, or observe the rubrics of the Prayer Book. Laud's opposition to the Puritans not only led many to emigrate on the *Mayflower* in 1620 to settle in America and there rigorously separate their Church from state controls, but also hastened the Civil War and the abolition of episcopacy by the Long Parliament. Injustice, however, occurred on all sides. When the Puritans came into power under Cromwell they were just as intolerant as Laud had been: Presbyterianism was imposed by force upon the nation, use of the Book of Common Prayer was made a penal offence, the Anglican faith was suppressed by law, bishops were driven abroad, or into hiding in remote areas, churches were despoiled, and the observance of Christian feasts, such as Christmas, banned. Even the Puritan Richard Baxter (1615–91) was alarmed at the excesses of the Puritans:

The disorderly tumultuous cries and petitions of such ignorant zealots for extremes under the name of Reformation had so great a part in our sin and misery from 1641–1660, as I must give warning to posterity to avoid the like and love moderation.†

* Quoted in More and Cross, *Anglicanism*, SPCK, London, 1962, pp.103-4.
† Quoted in More and Cross, *Anglicanism*, p.li.

In short, such objections as those made by the framers of the Millenary Petition were relatively superficial, and were tokens of more serious reasons for conflict, in particular the interest many of them had in limiting the power of the Monarchy, and in instituting a Presbyterian form of Church government. The debate shifted to the more controversial ground of Church dogma. One instance of this was the dispute over the doctrine of predestination, which Scottish Calvinists tended to stress very strongly. A simplified version of this grim and sober doctrine is that it taught that only those whom God had chosen would gain salvation, and, by implication, that all others were predestined to damnation. There was little point in attempting to labour at a devout life, since salvation or damnation were already determined.

The spirit of this doctrine was clearly antithetical to classical Anglicanism, and indeed to the urbane temper of many of the scholars and thinkers of the period. Yet its rigorous logic had an intellectual, and perhaps emotional, appeal for a leader such as Cromwell, and, to some extent, for John Milton. It has also been suggested that Calvinism's determinism and belief in predestination, its image of God as a God of power and will, who ordered the universe according to inexorable laws of inscrutable rationality, was in harmony with the increased interest in science since it encouraged the attempt to observe phenomena in order to understand something of the divine plan.

The Jesuits

Founded by Ignatius Loyola (1491–1556) in 1540 the Society of Jesus was, by the seventeenth century, a most potent influence in Europe and England, and was the unchallenged leader of the Counter-Reformation. The key feature of the order was its aggressive proselytising: the *Spiritual Exercises* of Ignatius formed the basis of Jesuit devotional life, and were designed to fix upon every Jesuit a deep sense of the personal leadership of Christ, and a determination to establish a universal Church under one head, the Pope. This massive vision had enormous political implications. To aid its implementation the Jesuits actively involved themselves in all the intellectual and artistic interests of the period: all human activity was to be consecrated to the greater glory of God. In this sense the vision of the Jesuits, their active engagement with art and thought, facilitated the development of the Baroque style in art.

The impact of the Jesuits upon England in the seventeenth century was considerable. Anti-papal feeling in England was influenced both by the political events of the time, such works as the *Book of Martyrs* (1559 and 1563) by John Foxe (1516–87) and by the militant Catholicism of the Counter-Reformation. The missions of the English Jesuits from their College at Douai in the 1580s to succour the recusants and convert the English to Roman Catholicism epitomised this militancy, and many of these priests were executed, including the Jesuit poet Robert Southwell. Until the Gunpowder Plot, James I was inclined to be tolerant, but in 1604 the expulsion of Catholic clergy from England was ordered, and Roman Catholics were subsequently required to take an Oath of Allegiance to the Throne.

Devotional life: techniques and literary influences

A legacy from the Reformation and Counter-Reformation, and an aspect of Renaissance thought, was a strong degree of introspection in religious life. Religious practices moulded habits of reflection and their application may suggest the imaginative influence of the drama. The seventeenth century saw a flowering of various forms of religious writings: pamphlets, tracts, collections of sermons and manuals. These frequently contained advice on meditation and how to contemplate the principal religious mysteries, particularly those related to the life of Christ, or the state of one's soul. Traditions evolved, Jesuit, Franciscan, Augustinian, Salesian, Puritan, to help the individual to order his faith better. In Europe the writings of St Ignatius Loyola, Teresa of Avila (1515–82), St John of the Cross (1542–91) and Francis de Sales (1567–1622) had a powerful effect, while in England Donne, Lancelot Andrewes (1555–1626), Nicholas Ferrar (1592–1637), Richard Baxter and Jeremy Taylor (1613–67) were the best-known influences.

The introspection of Metaphysical poetry may owe more to the habits of meditation in the period than to the example of Donne. Most forms of meditation involved the 'three powers of the soul': memory, understanding and will. A devotional subject would be chosen, such as the Annunciation, the Crucifixion, the Four Last Things—death, judgement, hell and heaven—or some object in nature, and the subject would be developed with the faculties of mind and imagination. Two basic strategies for this were called 'composition of place' and 'composition by similitude'. Composition of place required the meditator to imagine the scene vividly, perhaps even putting himself in it. Composition by similitude required that the meditator should take an abstraction—death, sin—and give it substance through a concrete image. So, for example, Hamlet picks up a skull as the tangible image of death and soliloquises on that. The end result is a colloquy in which emotions and emphatic resolutions are formed and expressed as a result of the meditation.

Many of the Metaphysical poets follow a structure which resembles the techniques advocated in various meditative traditions, particularly when dealing with religious subjects. Probably the most influential of the writers on meditative techniques was Ignatius Loyola who compiled the *Spiritual Exercises*. This book is essentially a manual on meditation. Loyola takes the classical faculties of the mind—memory, understanding and will—and uses them to induce a receptiveness to mystical experience. The Ignatian tripartite scheme of memory, intellect and will can be traced in many of the poems of Donne and Herbert: first the 'memory' is involved in a vivid and dramatic 'composition of place' which imaginatively reconstructs a devotional subject; second, point by point, comes the intellectual analysis of the subject; finally there is the concluding 'colloquy' or address to God with its emphatic and emotional conclusion. Other models were also popular. The Salesian method which emphasises the mutuality of love between God and Man, and urges abandonment of self to God, influences some of Crashaw's work, while the influence of St Augustine (AD354–430), St Bernard (1090–1153) and St Bonaventura (1221–74) can be traced in Marvell, Vaughan and Traherne.

In an age of religious earnestness other forms of devotion also made their impression. The forms of vocal devotion, most clearly represented in the Book of Common Prayer, were as vital as the forms of meditation and contemplation: in particular the Church's liturgy of the Holy Communion, the forms of Morning and Evening Prayer, the elaborate Hymnology and varied uses and settings of the Psalms. So, for example, Donne wrote three hymns, and Herbert's works—such as 'Easter'—demonstrate his interests in psalmody. In his *Life of Herbert*, Izaak Walton (1593 – 1683) recalls that on his last Sunday alive, Herbert rose from his sick bed and sang a stanza of his poem 'Sunday' while accompanying himself on the viol. Vaughan wrote some holy-day hymns, the best known of which is 'Ascension-day', and Crashaw's hymns are especially appealing, 'In The Holy Nativity' being most attractive.

Chapter 2

The variety of Metaphysical poetry and poets

The literary background

A sense of the literary developments of Renaissance England is essential if the Metaphysical poets are to be understood in context. Literature feeds off, and develops from, the examples of preceding writers. The plays of Shakespeare owe much to ancient popular drama; Jacobean and Caroline poetry builds upon the achievements and conventions of the Elizabethans. The various literary traditions of the seventeenth century do not exist in watertight compartments. Ben Jonson and his 'sons' popularised the elegant 'Cavalier' fashion, Donne and Herbert the tense intellectual style of the Metaphysicals. The extent to which poets crossed traditions, and the artificiality of critical divisions, are illustrated by the way Jonson could occasionally sound like Donne, and vice versa, while Milton sounded like neither.

Prose

Donne's sermons remind us that the seventeenth century was not simply dominated by Metaphysical poetry. Initially, by its imitation of ancient Greek and Roman authors, English humanism had followed the classicism of the Renaissance. But the Renaissance humanists were liberal in their attitude to language and enriched the vernacular English by Latin borrowings, and there was a gradual increase in interest in the use of vernacular. This can be seen in the number of European and classical works translated into English, the translation into English of works by English humanists who had originally written in Latin, and such major vernacular works as Tyndale's (d.1536) Bible (1525–31). By the 1580s Sir Philip Sidney (1554–86) advocated the use of classical metres in English poetry, and in drama Shakespeare (1564–1616) demonstrated the resources of the native tongue. The vernacular thrust culminated in 1660 with the foundation of the Royal Society and its efforts to standardise the English language. Classical literary models, however, rebuilt the use of English prose throughout the sixteenth and seventeenth centuries, with Cicero the original model—elaborate, balanced, ornate, with many dependent clauses and rounded periods—epitomised in *Euphues, the Anatomy of Wit* (1578) by John Lyly (*c.*1554–1606). By the seventeenth century the lively, short sentences of Seneca (*c.*5BC–AD65), and the variations of pace and style of his thought, were a more popular influence.

In Europe Montaigne had demonstrated that prose was an instrument for intellectual exploration. In England, the crisp gnomic wisdom of Bacon, and the clear common sense of Hobbes, the elegant style of Thomas Browne, or the polished theological prose of Richard Hooker in his *Laws of Ecclesiastical Polity* (1594), did likewise. Geographical exploration and speculation was provided by Richard Hakluyt (1552–1616) whose monumental account of discoveries, *Principall Navigations, Voiages, and Discoveries of the English Nation* (1589), reflected the curiosity of the age just as John Lyly's *Euphues* provided a gilded artificial style of expression which, often copied and parodied by literary gallants, reflected a delight in the elaborate. This was also a pamphleteering age: religious, political and satirical pamphleteering thrived. Perhaps the most notable of such writers was Thomas Nashe (1567–1601). Many pamphlets issued at this time reflected popular hostility to bishops or Puritans, and are remarkable for their racy style, forceful language and vivid imagination, powers of description and imagery.

Drama

From the private halls of the Inns of Court, the outdoor theatre built in 1576, and the various public enclosed theatres that sprang up about London until the Puritans closed the theatres in 1642, a superb dramatic tradition evolved from the foundations of Elizabethan theatre with its blend of native vernacular and classical learned traditions.

It was a period of immense variety, with drama ranging from the great public plays of the Globe to the private, learned and now largely lost masques of the Court of James I. While some acting companies attached themselves to individual aristocrats, others became established with particular theatres, and, as a result, these theatres often took on a very individual complexion, being associated with specific playwrights, audiences and styles of presentation. A variety of great talents were attracted: from the heavily witty Thomas Dekker (*c.*1570–1632), to the learned and neoclassical Ben Jonson. Drama provided a public forum which shaped, as it was shaped by, the taste of the age. We are told by Walton that Donne in his youth was 'a great frequenter of plays', and even a casual reader will be impressed by the darkness of the Jacobean tragedies such as those of John Webster and Cyril Tourneur (?1575 – 1626) and of the way their spirit suggests Burton's (1577 – 1640) *Anatomy of Melancholy* (1621) or Donne's later death-haunted poems.

From the drama of the period we can trace the tradition of soliloquy, wit, punning and surprise that are found in the work of the Metaphysical poets and which suggest their propinquity to it. For example, in certain of the poems, most notably the *Satires*, Donne approximates the persona of the malcontent and rails at life, convention and cant. Or again, his abrupt openings mark a strong sense of dramatic context, as if we are coming suddenly upon an argument between contenders. While the influence of the drama may have influenced the development of the surprise opening as a poetic device, the number of its occurrences is remarkable. A good instance of this is 'The Canonization' where Donne begins 'For Godsake hold your tongue, and let me love,/ Or chide my palsie, or my gout . . .'. This characteristic explains why readers find it so easy to remember the opening lines of many of Donne's poems. Such verbal blows as 'For Godsake hold your tongue, and let me love', or 'Batter my heart, three-person'd God' are not merely surprising, they are unforgettable. The technique is not, of course, restricted to Donne. Herbert employs it quite commonly, though usually to different effect, as in 'The Collar' with his 'I struck the board, and cry'd, No more.'

Poetry

During the late sixteenth and early seventeenth centuries an extraordinary number of literary forms were created, while well-established courtly and popular forms such as the masque and madrigal vanished under the pressures of social and political changes. In the first decade of the seventeenth century Elizabethan attitudes in literature continued. These attitudes included the conventions of the Petrarchan conceit in love poetry, so named for its association with the Italian poet Petrarch, which was characterised by exaggerated comparisons to celebrate, on the one hand, the haughtiness and desirability of a woman, and, on the other, the sufferings of her lover. The conventions, in particular the tendency to stereotype the catalogues of feminine charms and lovers' woes, made them vulnerable to parody—as in Marvell's 'To His Coy Mistress'—but remained a formative influence for the poets of this period. As for love sonnets and sonnet sequences, these had been the rage under Elizabeth I, but Donne turned the form to religious purposes and by Milton's time the form had faded from favour. It was a similar situation where allegorical poetry was concerned. The styles of Spenser (?1552–99), Sidney and Gascoigne

(?1539–77) can be recognised in the 'Spenserianism' of writers such as Daniel (1562–1619) or Fulke Greville (1554–1628) or Drayton: this mythological interest reached a climax in the radical Protestantism of Milton's *Paradise Lost*, and then faded with Dryden whose *The Hind and the Panther* turned it into burlesque.

On the surface, during the seventeenth century, poetry tended to become more regular in metre, and the influence of blank verse, brilliantly demonstrated by Shakespeare, receded. The most distinctive form employed was the rhymed couplet, a regular metre which enhanced the sense of mental play and verbal debate. This metre ultimately carried the witty antitheses of Augustanism, which were foreshadowed in the seventeenth-century's most fashionable style, the verse satire, which increased in its range and subtlety.

A taste for difficulty

In his influential preface to Ovid's *Banquet of Sense* (1595) where plainness of expression was considered 'the plain way to barbarism', Chapman had made difficulty a test of poetic merit and his view marks a conscious reaction against what was felt to be the looseness of style and thought in much Elizabethan poetry. The vogue of satire and the popularity of the epigram demonstrate this change in taste and circumstances. English satire was initially associated with the Inns of Court, especially John Marston. Marston's Ovidian satires emulated the Roman poet's witty brevity and antitheses to explore the tension between the Petrarchan ideal of love and human reality. The difficult, abrupt style of his *Certaine Satyres* (1598) and *The Scourge of Villanie* (1598) was modelled on the Roman satirist Persius (AD34–62), and his malcontent narrator anticipates the stance of many of Donne's *Songs and Sonnets*.

The coarse, harshly satirical examples of Martial (*c.*AD40–*c.*104) provided the classical model for the epigram. Not confined to the Metaphysicals, its exponents blended witty brevity with a more personal quality which reflected the compact literary milieu of the time— namely their occasional address to individuals. A remarkable variety of expression could be achieved, ranging from the delicate compliments of Robert Herrick to the brutal barbs of Donne and Jonson. Donne's 'Disinherited' demonstrates that such compression could be both sharp-tongued in attack, and agile in thought:

> Thy father all from thee, by his last will,
> Gave to the poor; thou hast good title still.

And this robust example from Ben Jonson on a moral theme ('On Gut') but with, probably, a personal target in mind:

Gut eats all day, and lechers all the night;
  So all his meat he tasteth over, twice;
And striving so to double his delight,
  He makes himself a thoroughfare of vice.
Thus in his belly can he change a sin:
  Lust it comes out, that gluttony went in.*

A small circle of poets

The place of poetry in seventeenth-century society as a social accomplishment was analogous to that of music. From Elizabethan times English courtly society had a rich musical culture: its madrigals, airs and ballads were enriched by folk songs, and enlivened by forms from the Continent; and, much as with fencing, hunting and Latin, music was a major social accomplishment expected of gentlemen. So with poetry. In this intimate social context it was an art of gracious social expression, and usually written with a particular audience in mind. These poems were designed to be handed about in manuscripts for the amusement of friends; they were not initially intended for publication. In the phrase of the professional, Drayton, the authors of these poems were 'Chamber poets', and their writing has the characteristics of the coterie—both its strengths and weaknesses.

Much of this can be demonstrated from Donne's *Songs and Sonnets*. Most expressive of an intimate social context is the vitality drawn from a bustling court and urban life: the urgency of a lover hurrying a woman to undress, the cursing of an enemy, or the contempt for a mistress's husband run through these early poems. On some occasions it seems that the poet is excessively intent upon proving his own wit by surprising or even shocking his readers, and that the influence (and expectation) of a circle of admirers has dominated. This is balanced by the ease with which Donne can assume the support, interest and tolerance of his intimate audience—it allows, even encourages him to be innovative. Dominating all is a poetic persona whose intense vision, whose personal address, and whose purpose are intended to amuse the reader as well as demonstrate the poet's wit.

Characteristics of Metaphysical poetry

Modern criticism

Modern criticism of the Metaphysicals dates from Grierson's anthology and T.S. Eliot's praise of their fusion of thought and feeling. Though

* Quoted in T.G.S. Cain (ed.), *Jacobean and Caroline Poetry: An Anthology*, Methuen, London, 1981, p.59.

subject to intensive scrutiny, Metaphysical poetry has fared well with later critics: some have remarked on the Metaphysicals' expression of Renaissance individualism, namely that they present a private, not a public, world. Many have concentrated upon stylistic features: recondite imagery, dissonance, logical argumentative structure, equivocal nature, dramatic qualities. Most favoured of all has been the view that 'wit'—imaginative intelligence shown in verbal and intellectual agility —is a defining characteristic.

Recent studies point to the limitations of 'metaphysical' as a broad description and remind us that the various facets of the cultural scene were closely intertwined. For example the distinctions between 'Metaphysicals' and 'Classicals' blur when particular poems, genres, or individual poets are the issue. In support of this the variety of poems produced by Marvell can be mentioned: the 'Horatian Ode upon Cromwel's Return from Ireland' is clearly 'classical', while 'On a Drop of Dew' displays metaphysical wit. Other cultural factors then assume importance, such as the practices of religious meditation with their influence on poetic structure; the common influence of rhetorical theory and practice; or the interest in a 'plain style' demonstrated by both Donne and Jonson; the influence of European culture upon English writers; the 'genre-consciousness' of the age and its influence upon style.

What seems to have forced this later much debated description of the poetry of Donne and many of his contemporaries is its distinctiveness from what had gone before. Donne did not initiate the break with Petrarchanism, but in his poetry the change of taste occasionally foreshadowed by various Elizabethan writers—whether in the occasional sonnets of Shakespeare where lyrical ease is tempered by Renaissance perturbation with its stylistic inversions and poses, or Sir John Davies in the mock Petrarchanism of his Gulling Sonnets—is carried to an extreme. The degree of this contrast with the sweet sounds and Petrarchan conventions of Elizabethan verse, and the extent to which it is a conscious manner, define the style.

Various stylistic features remind us that Donne was himself an Elizabethan, and show the extent to which Metaphysical poetry evolved from Elizabethan literary traditions. For example, two major points of any poetry are sound and imagery. In Donne's case the mere sound of his poems, and their use of figurative language, especially their conceits, are two elements which not only provide vivid demonstration of how the Metaphysicals inherited stylistic conventions, commonplaces and assumptions from their Elizabethan predecessors, but also show how they developed characteristics which became particularly their own. Amongst these distinctive features of the Metaphysical style its compression should particularly be noted. Consistently complex allusions and implications are expressed with a verbal economy which can, on occasions, appear cryptic. Beyond this are the various dimensions of 'wit'—a word often used and various in its meanings (see below, p.38). For the Metaphysical style any definition will have its limitations, but the sense of a lively intelligence is paramount and it may be expressed in a variety of ways: the vigorous play upon words; the startling correlations of knowledge, experience and particular situations or objects which may often be grotesque or bizarre, or the dramatic poses and terms of address. The list is not exclusive, but all these features mark a shift in literary style so major that near contemporaries were able to speak of a 'School of Donne'.

Sound

The Renaissance connection of music with poetry reflected its emulation of classical culture. Just as in classical literature the Latin writers imitated the literary distinctions and conventions of the ancient Greeks, for whom lyric poetry was traditionally erotic and associated with music as song, so the Renaissance sought to re-unite poetry and music and this close association of the two art forms continued into the seventeenth century. In the 1580s England abounded with musical settings of poetic texts. For all poets one of the great commonplaces was the idea of *harmonia mundi*, a universal harmony in creation of which music was the emblem; related concepts underlie poems such as Vaughan's 'Morning Watch' and Crashaw's 'Musicks Duell', and recur throughout the poetry of the period from Spenser and Shakespeare to Milton and Dryden.

The musical nature of Elizabethan poetry, its 'sweet' style and mellifluous ease of expression, are its most obvious features. Technically this is accomplished through smooth flowing rhythms where there is little or no variation from the metrical norm. A good example of this comes from the collection of 'Songs and Sonnets' compiled by Richard Tottel (*c.*1530–94) known as *Tottel's Miscellany*. In this work Wyatt's (?1503–42) lyric 'They flee from me, that sometime did me seek', is 'smoothed' to comply with Elizabethan taste. The original in the Egerton MS reads as follows in the first seven lines:

> They flee from me, that sometime did me seek,
> With naked foot, stalking in my chamber;
> I have seen them gentle, tame, and meek,
> That now are wild and do not remember
> That sometime they put themself in danger
> To take bread at my hand; and now they range,
> Busily seeking with a continual change*

* Quoted in Geoffrey G. Hiller (ed.), *Poems of the Elizabethan Age: An Anthology*, Methuen, London, 1977, p.89.

In Tottel's miscellany the taste for mellifluousness takes over and the spirit of the poem is marred by the adjustments made to its metre and language. In this version the iambic pattern is more obvious:

> They flee from me, that sometime did me sake
> With naked fote stalkying within my chamber.
> Once have I seen them gentle, tame, and meke,
> That now are wild, and do not once remember
> That sometyme they have put themselves in danger,
> To take bread at my hand, and now they range,
> Busily sekyng in continuall change.

The greater regularity of sound in this second version of the poem is immediately clear when it is read aloud. But there is more to it than this: the 'sense' of the poem has also been amended to complement the regularity of its rhythm. 'Meaning' has been sacrificed to 'sound' and a sense of art and studied grace dominate; there are no hidden 'snags', twists of thought, or reversals. The work stands complete, unequivocal and assured in sharp contrast to the often tortured equivocations of Metaphysical poetry.

The contrast of sound between a poem in the 'sweet' Spenserian fashion and a Metaphysical work is readily demonstrated. Take, for example, these lines from a sonnet by Samuel Daniel:

> Care-charmer Sleepe, sonne of the sable Night,
> Brother to death, in silent darknes borne,
> Relieve my languish, and restore the light,
> With darke forgetting of my care's, returne.*

The smoothness, or 'sweetness', of these lines is in sharp contrast with the characteristically abrupt colloquial opening of these lines from Donne's 'Love's Deity'. The difference of sound is not merely a matter of subject, but rather is due to a fundamental difference of approach:

> I long to talk with some old lover's ghost,
>   Who died before the god of love was born:
> I cannot think that he, who then loved most,
>   Sunk so low, as to love one which did scorn.

Because Donne based his rhythms upon colloquial speech of the time and took care to notate his manuscripts accordingly, early printed editions attempted to represent where vowels were slurred or elided by using apostrophes or contractions such as ''twere', 'swol'n', ''gainst'. Here the sound is inseparable from the rhythm of the poem. We are struck by the absence of convention, or cliché, and are 'button-

---

* Quoted in Maurice Evans (ed.), *Elizabethan Sonnets*, Dent, London, 1977, p.83.

holed' by the poet, who creates the sense of a personal and highly individual voice addressing us.

The description of Donne's poetry as 'Songs and Sonnets', with its allusion to music, underlines his dependence upon, and also his departure from, Elizabethan models. His tense, wrenched and idiosyncratic rhythms made setting to music almost impossible. It appears he may have had little concern about this. In 'The Triple Fool' he cynically refers to the musician as one whose 'art and voice to show / Doth set and sing my pain'. The fact, of course, is that with Donne a massive shift of emphasis has occurred in the way the text of the poem is perceived and used. Now sound, especially musical setting, is supplanted by the speaking voice, the verbal 'music' provided by the poet's intense speech cadences.

In short, sound sharply distinguishes the poetry of the Metaphysicals. But this is not incidental: this roughness of sound and use of an idiomatic speech rhythm expresses a different attitude to experience. In contrast to the lyrical grace of the Spenserians, the dramatic tones and rhythms of a natural speaking voice demonstrate a new realism. While the Metaphysicals could, and did, write with great concern for form and subtlety of metre and rhyme, they often intended that the verse should be rough, rugged or irregular. As such it drew the fire of distinguished critics and practitioners of poetry. The other great poetic figure of the time, Ben Jonson, thought Donne 'deserved hanging' for the way he was indifferent to accent. More restrained, another contemporary, Izaak Walton in his *Compleat Angler* (1653), referred to this feature of the style as 'strong lines'—thereby providing a phrase that has stuck.

The conceit

Favoured alike by the Elizabethans and the Metaphysicals, probably the most commented-upon device of the poetry of the Metaphysicals is the conceit, which, as with sound, demonstrates a shift in use and style. In sharp contrast to the decorative conceits characteristic of Elizabethan writing, the Metaphysical conceit is organic rather than decorative: that is to say, it embodies and develops the thought rather than merely embellishes it. Designed to define or persuade, it represents an extreme proof by analogy and forces speculation: its dramatic, rigorous, complex and unlikely analogies express its rhetorical intention. The result is a style in which nothing can be taken for granted and where subject, tone, professed attitudes and sentiments are all equivocal. In fact, a distorted or unexpected perspective is almost the essence of the Metaphysical conceit. Samuel Johnson recognised this in his memorably pithy and often quoted image for the sense of strain which characterises this feature of Metaphysical figurative language. He refers to the poet's 'wit' as a 'kind of *discordia concors*, a combination of dissimilar images, or discovery of occult resemblances in things apparently unlike.'*

Take, for example, two poems of the same 'species': Donne's 'Good Morrow' and that with the same title by George Gascoigne. Both mark a consciousness of genre: they are aubades, poems welcoming the day. Gascoigne links the rainbow with the promise of redemption:

> The rainbow bending in the sky,
> Bedecked with sundry hues,
> Is like the seat of God on high,
> And seems to tell these news:
> That as thereby he promisëd
> To drown the world no more,
> So by the blood which Christ hath shed
> He will our health restore.

The effect of this image is generally reassuring. Its pleasure for us lies in our recognition of the subject—although a commonplace and in no way testing the intellect. By contrast, Donne's opening conceit is personal, idiosyncratic and equivocal:

> I wonder by my troth, what thou, and I
> Did, till we loved? were we not weaned till then,
>   But sucked on country pleasures, childishly?
>   Or snorted we in the seven sleepers' den?
>   'Twas so; but this, all pleasures fancies be.
>   If ever any beauty I did see,
> Which I desired, and got, 'twas but a dream of thee.

The immediate effect of the conceit here is far from reassuring. The controlling image of infancy and physical love—as 'got' makes quite clear, this love is also physical—momentarily shocks and then challenges the reader to determine just what Donne means. The conceit does not immediately clarify or yield its meaning. Does it mean 'the spiritual depth of my love for you shows all my previous carnal loves to be immature as a babe?' Or does the poet mean 'Before I loved you I did not know the physical possibilities of love, my women were only dreams?'

A useful approach is to distinguish two broad categories of conceits: those which condense an idea radically and those which are extended through an entire poem or several stanzas. A concise example of the former is Donne's allusion to 'A bracelet of bright hair about the

* James Boswell, *Life of Johnson*, p.678.

bone' in 'The Relic' where we are shocked by the different and strongly contrasted associations evoked by 'bright hair' and 'bone'. In the sequence of Holy Sonnets known as *La Corona*, the second sonnet dealing with the Annunciation reflects the technique of condensation as Donne speaks of the Virgin having *'Immensity cloistered in thy dear womb'*. Reminiscent of this meditation, a more sustained example of the condensed conceit is Crashaw's 'In The Holy Nativity of Our Lord God: A Hymn Sung as by the Shepheards':

Wellcome, all WONDERS in one sight!
   Æternity shutt in a span.
Sommer in Winter. Day in Night.
   Heauen in earth, & GOD in MAN.
Great little one! whose all-embracing birth
Lifts earth to heauen, stoops heau'n to earth.

The movement of the metaphor is inwards and downwards. The cosmos is drawn into the person of the infant Christ. Past, present and future, the fullness of eternity, all are concentrated in this particularity. While using the commonplace paradoxes of religious thought Crashaw gives fresh insight by the intensity of his expression as aspects of the one theme are progressively explored and ideas set against each other.

A memorable example of an expanded conceit is in Donne's 'A Valediction: forbidding Mourning' where grief at the parting of lovers is overcome by a conceit which is developed through several successive stanzas and which assures the lovers of their continuing spiritual union:

Our two souls therefore, which are one,
   Though I must go, endure not yet
A breach, but an expansion,
   Like gold to aery thinness beat.

If they be two, they are two so
   As stiff twin compasses are two,
Thy soul the fixed foot, makes no show
   To move, but doth, if th' other do.

And though it in the centre sit,
   Yet when the other far doth roam,
It leans, and hearkens after it,
   And grows erect, as that comes home.

Such wilt thou be to me, who must
   Like th' other foot, obliquely run;
Thy firmness makes my circle just,
   And makes me end, where I begun.

The essential movement of the conceit is outwards. From the assessment of the relationship of the lovers in the metaphor 'like gold to aery thinness beat', the sense of expansion rather than fragmentation is established. The conceit of the compasses is integral to this controlling idea. The terms of the geometer's compass denote the lovers: as one moves, so the other, the fixed term of the compass, 'leans, and hearkens after it', while the indissoluble spiritual union of the lovers is denoted by the jointure of the compasses above the plane of the paper.

Argument and persuasion

An intellectual quality is an equally compelling feature of poetry written by Donne, Herbert and Marvell. Invariably the demand is made of the reader that the connection of ideas be grasped. The reader is held to a line of argument, a sequence of thought, where every stage of development must be accurately followed and understood if the poem is to make sense. Here, for example, is one of Donne's 'Holy Sonnets':

> If poisonous minerals, and if that tree,
> Whose fruit threw death on else immortal us,
> If lecherous goats, if serpents envious
> Cannot be damned; alas, why should I be?
> Why should intent or reason, born in me,
> Make sins, else equal, in me more heinous?
> And mercy being easy, and glorious
> To God, in his stern wrath, why threatens he?
> But who am I, that dare dispute with thee
> O God? Oh! of thine only worthy blood,
> And my tears, make a heavenly lethean flood,
> And drown in it my sin's black memory;
> That thou remember them, some claim as debt,
> I think it mercy, if thou wilt forget. (Sonnet 9)

That this poem provides us with an argument is clearly demonstrated by the conditional and polemical 'If' with which it opens. In the octave (the first eight lines) the speaker argues against a divine justice that makes capacity for reason and choice the factor which enables 'damnation'. Donne argues from nature against God: he enumerates occasions of supposed evil in the natural world, and, from the implication that reason and choice are part of the natural order, complains that divine justice is unjust since it damns him for something with which he was born. The dispute in the octave is completed by an argument drawn from the nature of God himself, namely the divine attribute of mercy: Donne feels that God's failure to be merciful is inconsistent with his divine nature. Most noticeable are the tight sequence of ideas and the witty twists of thought which the reader must follow closely and unravel with care. Apart from the sestet (the last six lines) which turns back against the questions in the octave from another perspective, the whole poem can be seen as an intellectual puzzle in which the poet debates within himself.

Perhaps the best and most famous example of a Metaphysical poem as an exercise in witty reasoning is Donne's poem 'The Flea'. Here the argument is a clever syllogism which pretends to trap the unwary listener who accepts the analogies or premises Donne offers. He delights the reader by his daring analogies, but in particular by his ingenuity in making so much out of so little:

> Mark but this flea, and mark in this,
> How little that which thou deny'st me is;
> Me it sucked first, and now sucks thee,
> And in this flea, our two bloods mingled be;
> Confess it, this cannot be said
> A sin, or shame, or loss of maidenhead,
>   Yet this enjoys before it woo,
>   And pampered swells with one blood made of two,
>   And this, alas, is more than we would do.

> Oh stay, three lives in one flea spare,
> Where we almost, nay more than married are.
> This flea is you and I, and this
> Our marriage bed, and marriage temple is;
> Though parents grudge, and you, we'are met,
> And cloistered in these living walls of jet.
>   Though use make you apt to kill me,
>   Let not to this, self murder added be,
>   And sacrilege, three sins in killing three.

> Cruel and sudden, hast thou since
> Purpled thy nail, in blood of innocence?
> In what could this flea guilty be,
> Except in that drop which it sucked from thee?
> Yet thou triumph'st, and say'st that thou
> Find'st not thyself, nor me the weaker now;
>   'Tis true, then learn how false, fears be;
>   Just so much honour, when thou yield'st to me,
>   Will waste, as this flea's death took life from thee.

The premise upon which the poet bases his argument is a dexterous analogy between a flea bite, with the mixture of bloods in one flea, and the nature of sexual intercourse and the theology of marriage. From this equation he elaborates a flashing word-play which makes the flea the sacramental agency of their union and suggests that their lives, and even children, are bound up within the flea. As an exercise in philosophical sleight of hand the poem appeals by its audacity and by its challenge to the reader to argue with the speaker.

Wit and concentration

In Metaphysical poetry expansive elegance is subordinated to contracted forms which emphasise meaning and ingenuity. This shift of emphasis accords with those aspects of Renaissance literary taste which valued complexity, 'artifice', and poetry as a demonstration of 'wit'. Consequently its broken rhythms and colloquial speech, use of figurative language for debate rather than ornament, and its rigorous intellectual realism can all be located within an aesthetic which esteemed that concentrated meaning and witty economy of expression which differentiates the Metaphysicals from the Elizabethans. A remark in a sermon upon the Psalms reflects the value Donne sets upon economy, 'where all words are numbered, and measured, and weighed, the whole work is less subject to falsification'.*

The meaning of the term 'wit' changed considerably in the course of the seventeenth century. Initially it denoted the intellectual and spiritual faculties which discerned coherence in the great mix of experience. Of this usage Donne is the best example. In his works the clash of knowledge between the old scholasticism and the possibilities suggested by humanism and the new sciences is held in imaginative balance by the wit of his poetic artifice. By the mid-century, however, 'wit' had diminished to mean cleverness in an antithetical style, and its place as a cohering principle in art was supplanted by 'sense'. By the eighteenth century wit had degenerated into marking a talent for bawdy repartee and *double entendre*.

The tendency to compression suggests a restlessness, uncertainty and energy, a desire to identify and comprehend essentials. It can be discerned in various ways. For example, the new use of the conceit as a means of argument generally intensified the concentration of meaning. On the other hand, not only do harshness of sound and expression voice a general sense of intellectual tension, but the cramped taut nature of the diction dramatically enforces it. By sheer economy of language, each word, image and line is forced to carry the maximum weight of meaning.

Good poetry seldom yields all its meaning at once. Metaphoric

* Evelyn M. Simpson and George R. Potter, *The Sermons of John Donne*, 10 vols, University of California Press, Berkeley and Los Angeles, 1984, Vol. II, p.50.

thought cuts through the processes of formal systematic reasoning, sometimes radically condensing those processes to a line or an image, and allows the poet to express an insight, a new way of seeing or understanding things, by his arbitrary association of dissimilar phenomena. A reward of such writing is the sense of discovery or recognition experienced when a poem gradually opens to our understanding.

This certainly applies to the Metaphysical poets. On the one hand, not only are the Metaphysicals difficult because they reflect an unfamiliar view of the world, but the Metaphysical style, with its implications and witty concentration, compounds obscurities and difficulties for the reader or listener. This has to be related to the role of wit and what the poet (perhaps rather flatteringly) considered he could expect of his readers. In many instances the challenge is that we are left to work out the connection between the images the poet has combined. A challenge of that sort invariably has the effect of ensuring the reader's attention—and, in a light-hearted way, this is, of course, what 'The Flea' achieves. Donne twists and weaves with an idea, follows possibilities, analogies and variations, but seldom lets the poem become slackened by a careless usage. Everything has been chosen with care and we are forced to follow him closely if we are fully to understand him. Yet wit has its serious aspects too. For example, Donne's opening lines in 'The Dissolution' convey a dramatic feeling of urgency and a sense that it is important that the meaning should be understood. In the business of unravelling the meaning, the reader is, as it were, obliged to work out a puzzle:

She is dead; and all which die
    To their first elements resolve;
And we were mutual elements to us,
    And made of one another.

As these poems gradually elicit our understanding, our delight at a puzzle solved, and our pleasure in the sharpness of the poet's insight, skill and wit, are commensurate to our efforts in following it. As Jasper Mayne (1604–72) remarked in his elegy on Donne:

Wee are thought wits, when 'tis understood.

The boundaries of Metaphysical poetry

As the seventeenth century advanced, different modes or poetic traditions merged. Metaphysical poetry moved up from the Inns to the Court, and the Spenserian mode blended with the Cavalier lyric, while the neo-classical influence of Jonson and Edward Fairfax (?1580–1635) can be detected in the increasing use of heroic couplets, epistles and other formal kinds of verse. Many poets who admired both Donne's wit and Jonson's clarity, such as Thomas Carew, really belong within the class of the 'Cavalier poets'. The reason for this classification is essentially based upon the ease of expression to be found in these poets and in the noticeable lack of urgency in their poetry. Whereas with Donne or Herbert there is a sense of struggle and engagement, with the Cavalier poets there is a gracious facility of expression and a lack of engagement. Poetry has moved from the centre of life to the fringe as an elegant accomplishment.

The Cavalier poets: Carew, Lovelace, Suckling

Thomas Carew's poetry epitomises the style of courtly wit which replaced the Metaphysical mode and incorporated elements from the neo-classical style. Izaak Walton remembered him as 'a poet of note and a great libertine in his life and talke'. Carew's chequered career took him through Oxford, the Inns of Court, Europe and the Court, and his style incorporates elements from this wide variety of experiences such as European Baroque and Marinism, the style named after the Italian poet Giambattista Marino (1569–1625), whose richly sensual, mellifluous and often clotted style epitomises Continental Baroque and greatly influenced many poets (Crashaw is probably the most striking instance of Marino's pervasive influence). Marino's style can be summarised as one of 'over-ripeness is all'. While he employs the conceits and oxymorons, paradoxes and antitheses found in Metaphysical poetry, his use of them is distinctively Baroque: where Donne and Herbert are intellectual, Marino is sensual. His work is packed with sensuous and often cloying description, florid rhetoric and elaborate ornamentation, and he applies these devices to sacred poetry. Carew's poetry incorporates aspects of Marino's style; he also uses Donne's direct address, but his stance is less intense, more playful, and Petrarchan conventions are deployed against a pleasure-seeking realism. Carew disdains the 'puling Poets whine' of unrequited love and his sexual imagery is more euphemistic than figurative. This is shown, for example, in his poem 'To a Lady That Desired I Would Love Her':

> Rich Nature's store, (which is the poets treasure)
>   I'll spend, to dress
> Your beauties, if your mine of Pleasure
>   In equal thankfulness
> You but unlocke, so we each other bless.*

* Quoted in Thomas Clayton (ed.), *Cavalier Poets*, Oxford University Press, London, 1978, p.200.

Much the same can be said of Sir John Suckling, who borrows from Donne but adopts the tough-minded satire of Jonson in his cheerful and impertinent worldliness. In his verse the tone is often self-mocking, the diction plain, and poetry a witty game, as in 'The Constant Lover':

Out upon it, I have loved
  Three whole days together;
And am like to love three more,
  If it hold fair weather.*

Of the Cavalier poets the epitome of wit and courtliness is certainly Richard Lovelace. The author of some often quoted lines, his witty juxtapositions and concision are reminiscent of Donne, as in his 'To Lucasta, Going to the Wars':

True, a new mistress now I chase,
  The first foe in the field;
And with a stronger faith embrace
  A sword, a horse, a shield.†

Restoration wit: 'Clevelandism'

The coining of the term 'Clevelandism' is attributed to John Dryden and it denotes 'wresting and torturing a word into another meaning'. John Cleveland's (1613–58) poetry enjoyed considerable vogue in the mid-seventeenth century, and, although generally likened to Donne, his word play is clever in a flashy tortuous manner, without either Donne's engagement or his emotional and intellectual discipline. Here wit has degenerated into the topical, superficial and exaggerated satires associated with the university wits, and the taut intelligence of the main Metaphysical style has run to seed.

On the other hand, the wit of Abraham Cowley (1618–67) demonstrates the shift from a private world to a public style. His model is the Pindaric ode, named after the Greek lyric poet Pindar (518–438BC), and this extended form marks a different style of address and audience, and a more rational sensibility. Though his conceits faintly recall Donne, the vitality of the imagination is more constrained, and the poised analogies in such poems as his 'Ode: Of Wit', or 'On the Death of Mr Crashaw' indicate how much the Metaphysical style had merged with a neo-classical outlook.

* Quoted in Thomas Clayton (ed.), *Cavalier Poets*, Oxford University Press, London, 1978, p.200.
† Quoted in T.G.S. Cain (ed.), *Jacobean and Caroline Poetry: An Anthology*, Methuen, London, 1981, p.294.

Chapter 3

John Donne

An enigmatic and troubled life

Donne's style is the man. The witty fantasies, paradoxes and learning; the stark contrast between the various subjects of *Songs and Sonnets*, and the religious intensity of the *Divine Poems*, all these attracted comment during Donne's life, and still awaken curiosity today. His apparent metamorphosis from libertine to priest urges an explanation which intrigued critics still attempt. Dame Helen Gardner's division of the *Songs and Sonnets* into youthful libertine poems and the serious later poems demonstrates such an attempt to make sense of Donne's life and work, and explains the link between the 'libertine' Jack Donne of the Inns of Court and John Donne the devout Dean of St Paul's.

Gaps in our knowledge of Donne's life (1571/2–1631) make it difficult to date his poetry with any certainty. The comment of his contemporary Ben Jonson—probably an exaggeration—that Donne wrote 'all his best pieces ere he was 25 year old',* does not really help. However, it is widely accepted that Donne wrote very little poetry after his ordination in 1615, and that most of his poetry, including the *Holy Sonnets*, was written between 1590 and 1611. The notable exceptions to this are such occasional poems as 'Hymn to God my God, in my Sickness', 'A Hymn to God the Father' and 'Good Friday, 1613. Riding Westward'.

What biographical details we have are colourful and evocative. Born into a London merchant family with a Roman Catholic ancestry which included Sir Thomas More as his mother's great-grandfather, Donne studied at the University of Oxford and the Inns of Court. He left the former without taking the degree which would have required him to repudiate his Catholic ties by swearing the Oath of Allegiance. After travel in Europe and service abroad, which included the expedition to Cadiz with Raleigh and Essex in 1596, and a venture to the Azores in 1597, he found employment as secretary to Sir Thomas Egerton, whose niece, Ann More, he secretly married in 1601. Disgraced, dismissed from employment and briefly imprisoned, Donne supported his family on a hand to mouth basis in straitened circumstances. Between

* In 'Conversations with William Drummond of Hawthornden', in *Ben Jonson*, ed. C.H. Herford and Percy Simpson, Clarendon Press, Oxford, 1925, Vol. 1, p.135.

1602 and 1614 he made numerous attempts to secure state preferment, but was presumably handicapped by his Catholic ties. During these difficult years he clarified his religious views through a series of polemical publications against the Catholic Church, and, after his ordination (1615) and installation as Dean of St Paul's (1621), established a great reputation both for his preaching and his piety.

The secular poems

Introduction

Ben Jonson's assessment of Donne included the view that 'he was the first poet in the world for some things'. His style of wit was innovative and distinct. His immediacy, the tone of personal address from an urbane poetic persona, the densely loaded speech, the dramatic openings and gestures, and the impressive but often fantastic conceits, the general sense of a poetry hammered out of inner conflict, all win the admiration of modern readers.

Satires

Based upon the classical models of Persius, Horace (65–8BC) and Juvenal, Donne's *Satires* clearly reflect the Elizabethan satirical fashions of the 1590s: their harsh tone, their criticism of the vices and follies of the day, and a narrator who shares some characteristics of the malcontent. We can date these poems to about the period 1593–8 which makes them, with Joseph Hall's *Virgidemiarum* (1597), the first formal satires in English. Satire I, 'Away Thou Fondling Motley Humourist', is a brilliant and lively play upon the commonplace comparison between the contemplative and the active life. The poem vibrates with life. The student in his study at the Inns of Court—'this standing wooden chest'—castigates the creature of fashion who would lure him to pleasures in the streets, but yields—'Now we are in the street'. Details of fashion, street life, movement and speech are exactly caught and urge on the final moral twist.

Satires 2, 4 and 5 begin with the typical satirical fustian of the outraged moralist and they concern courtly and legal subjects. Satire 3 stands apart from them slightly since religion, though alluded to in the others, is now central. Although he is dealing with a highly controversial subject, Donne's attitude is urbane and tolerant. He skilfully contrasts trust in God with the bewildering variety of claims by Protestantism, Catholicism and Anglicanism, and defends a reasoned approach. The image of a search for authentic faith suggests Donne's own concerns and anticipates the prose works:

...doubt wisely, in strange way
To stand enquiring right, is not to stray;
To sleep, or run wrong is. On a huge hill,
Cragged, and steep, Truth stands, and he that will
Reach her, about must, and about must go;
And what the hill's suddenness resists, win so.*

Elegies

Contrary to our expectations, Donne's *Elegies* are not funeral poems but usually concern the relationship between a lover and his mistress. There are some textual problems which reflect the comparatively casual way in which it appears most of these poems were written and collected. For example, in most of the manuscripts these poems were not given titles, and those we know them by come from the second edition (1635). The *Elegies* belong to the 1590s; and the narrator—his wit, tone, imagery and vitality—echoes the narrator of the *Satires*. A representative example is 'To His Mistress Going to Bed': a witty celebration of the flesh, where Donne ingeniously expresses enjoyment of a new mistress through a conceit drawn from the new geographical discoveries:

Licence my roving hands, and let them go
Before, behind, between, above, below.
O my America, my new found land,
My kingdom, safeliest when with one man manned,
My mine of precious stones, my empery,
How blessed am I in this discovering thee!

The wit is very much that of Ovid's *Amores* in its desire to amuse and shock. That it succeeded can be indicated by the refusal of the licensing commissioners—a panel of churchmen—to allow five of the *Elegies* to be included in the first edition of Donne's poems (1633). In contrast to the *Satires*, the tone here is occasionally more calculated, disengaged and brutal, as in 'The Anagram' where the persona proposes what is clearly meant to be preposterous: marriage to a woman who 'Though all her parts be not in th' usual place, / She hath yet an anagram of a good face.' The philosophical sleight of hand which he employs later in a poem such as 'The Flea' is foreshadowed in 'The Anagram' when he remarks:

All love is wonder; if we justly do
Account her wonderful, why not lovely too?

* All quotations from Donne's poetry are from the edition by A.J. Smith, *John Donne: The Complete English Poems*, Penguin Books, Harmondsworth, 1971.

The break in the logic which he quickly passes over is, of course, that he does not also claim all that is wonderful to be lovable.

There is some question about the dates of these poems, for not all the *Elegies* have the same lightness of tone. While the claim 'All love is wonder' anticipates a serious view which is picked up in the 'First Anniversary' and 'A Valediction: of the Book', 'The Autumnal', which some manuscripts assign to the *Songs and Sonnets*, and others to the *Elegies*, is more serious in its witty treatment of mature beauty. Walton claims this was written for Magdalen Herbert. Donne's intellect moves past his subject as image piled upon image generates further associations. The amiable heat of his subject's eyes suggests a fever, then pestilence, then death. Leading on from this he says 'Call not these wrinkles, graves; if graves they were, / They were Love's graves', from which he evolves the idea of an anchorite, a religious recluse vowed to remain at a particular shrine.

Verse letters

Donne's numerous verse letters date from the years 1597–1614. They reflect the close intellectual milieu in which he wrote and the aristocratic world to which he had access through his wit, personal grace and talent for poetry. These were not intended for publication but are gracious and unconventional tributes to close friends or patronesses. The general manner of the verse letters reflects the witty economy of the epigrammatist, and the arrangement of verse couplets displays skill in a form which Pope (1688–1744) was to cultivate over a century later. 'The Storm' and 'The Calm' are both instances of a special form of rhetorical exercise—called *chronographia*—which was concerned with training in the art of detailed description, while those others written between 1597 and 1608 are generally brief experiments with a Horatian tone. Later letters frequently employ more serious forms of expression, though still with a courtly bravado; for example, the preposterous theological proposition he makes in his letter 'To the Countess of Bedford':

Reason is our soul's left hand, Faith her right,
By these we reach divinity, that's you . . .

Songs and Sonnets

Upon the *Songs and Sonnets* Donne's poetic reputation is founded: so distinctive is this collection of love lyrics in its forceful, witty imagination, energy and diversity of tone. Nonetheless these were not composed as a sequence or unified collection, and were not called *Songs and Sonnets* until so grouped by the editors of the 1635 edition, but represent the incidental work of perhaps twenty years. Indeed the attempt to find a consistent 'philosophy' within occasional poems written over a comparatively long period of time seems almost futile. Editors and critics have attempted to give some order to these isolated lyrics: some have looked for a unifying philosophy or central idea common to all; others have arranged them in groups according to subject, attitude and tone; others have wrestled with the vexed matter of dates; Helen Gardner combined these two latter approaches when she made the useful distinction between a group of poems which she dated to before 1600, and others written later than 1602, after Donne's marriage to Ann More.

While the poems extend the range of the Renaissance love lyric, they must be read in the context of the gradual change in taste away from the conventions of Elizabethan verse: on the one hand, the break with Petrarchanism is obvious, on the other hand Donne is clearly very much indebted to it—as his extreme use of hyperbole for emotional emphasis demonstrates. In short, at one level he is quite traditional, and, while poems such as 'Love's Alchemy' and 'The Blossom' mock spiritual love, most exploit aspects of the Renaissance conventions of love poetry. For example 'The Blossom' reflects the very conventional body-soul debates; 'The Apparition' demonstrates the lover's revenge on the Mistress whose indifference has killed him; the aubade, a dawn song which traditionally lamented the parting of lovers at the break of day, is represented by 'Break of Day'; 'The Flea' and 'Confined Love' clearly reflect the vigorous sensuality of Ovidian wit; and the subject of 'The Bait' recalls parallels in Marlowe and Raleigh.

On the formal level the *Songs and Sonnets* stand apart from the *Satires*, *Elegies* and *Anniversaries*. Instead of just employing the rhymed couplet, Donne now uses a great variety of stanza forms (though none of these is a sonnet proper). Stanza forms, tone and the number of lines and feet are dexterously varied, while the harshness of the lines is manipulated to catch a rhetorical emphasis. Originality is most obvious in Donne's adjustment of speech rhythms to express thought and make a unified appeal to mind and heart. In no other section of his poems is it quite so crucial to discriminate between his different voices and distinguish sincerity from entertaining flippancy.

The vigour of his language and his thought is consistent: he avoids abstractions by his direct argumentative engagement with the reader. The consequence is an implicit dialogue in which, while he uses a scholastic chop-logic, he also asserts the unity of body and spirit and demands that love be embodied. So too with his use of voice. His direct use of a semi-comic or serious dramatic monologue reinforces the sense of argument while allowing him also to catch the linguistic and social mannerisms of the time—and express them dramatically. As one critic has observed, 'Donne caught the tone of voice of the best company of his time in their hours of relaxation, in their private chambers: the ready learning and the instant wit, the generosity of praise and the cruelty of ridicule, the impudence and the flattery . . . '*.

The poems to which an early date has been attached—that is, pre-1600—are marked by a more relaxed tone, a streak of cynicism and the adopted pose of a libertine. What they generally demonstrate is wit as artifice, a skilful contrivance: these poems amuse by their ingenious intellectual manipulations but do not sound any intellectual or emotional depths. The attack upon Petrarchanism is obvious in the social monody† 'The Indifferent', where Donne draws upon Ovid's *Amores* (II.iv) for the catalogue of feminine charms, but parodies Petrarch's sighing lover. The third stanza is a witty burlesque of logic:

> Venus heard me sigh this song,
> And by love's sweetest part, variety, she swore,
> She heard not this till now; and that it should be so no more.
> She went, examined, and returned ere long,
> And said, 'Alas, some two or three
> Poor heretics in love there be,
> Which think to establish dangerous constancy.
> But I have told them, "Since you will be true,
> You shall be true to them, who are false to you."'

The flow of thought here is simple. Force of argument is achieved by irony: Venus supports variety, Petrarch's ideal of constancy in love is made—with a typical theological allusion—a heresy, and it is concluded that constant women are to be rewarded with inconstant men.

Close analysis of the entire poem shows that much of the force of Donne's argument depends upon its vehemence and repetition of key words or sounds which fix attention on his subject. There is a play upon the personal and relative pronouns, and a realistic balance between the antithetical metaphors 'abundance melts' and 'want betrays' in the first stanza; and there are persistent rhetorical questions in stanza two, which lead to the witty inversion of conventions in stanza three.

Another ingenious assault upon Petrarchan conventions occurs in 'Love's Deity'. Here Donne indulges a conventional Petrarchan complaint, the lament of a lover doomed to love a woman who does not reciprocate his affections:

---

* John Buxton. *Elizabethan Taste*, Macmillan, London, 1963, p.327.
† The conventional form for a lament, a famous example being Milton's *Lycidas* (1637).

I long to talk with some old lover's ghost,
  Who died before the god of love was born:
I cannot think that he, who then loved most,
  Sunk so low, as to love one which did scorn.
But since this god produced a destiny,
And that vice-nature, custom, lets it be;
  I must love her, that loves not me.

Sure, they which made him god, meant not so much,
  Nor he, in his young godhead practised it.
But when an even flame two hearts did touch,
  His office was indulgently to fit
Actives to passives. Correspondency
Only his subject was; it cannot be
  Love, till I love her, that loves me.

But every modern god will now extend
  His vast prerogative, as far as Jove.
To rage, to lust, to write to, to commend,
  All is the purlieu of the god of love.
Oh were we wakened by this tyranny
To ungod this child again, it could not be
  I should love her, who loves not me.

Rebel and atheist too, why murmur I,
  As though I felt the worst that love could do?
Love might make me leave loving, or might try
  A deeper plague, to make her love me too,
Which, since she loves before, I am loth to see;
Falsehood is worse than hate; and that must be,
  If she whom I love, should love me.

There are few obscurities in the argument. The secret of the poem's effect lies not in its content but in the urbane, meditative tone which holds our attention by the buttonholing strategy of the opening protest 'I long to talk with some old lover's ghost'. Donne imagines a lover in an ideal age before the birth of Cupid. He then shows how, in this lesser age, a mischievous Cupid has abused his powers and produced discords, with the result that the perverse ploy of today's courtly lovers is 'to rage, to lust, to write to, to commend'. But real love, Donne argues, is mutual. This simple—but incisive—perception turns the poet's 'complaint' back against himself; he concludes that he will not seek the woman's love since that would require that she should be false to another. On the surface this clinching 'reversal' against the conventions of the 'complaint' suggests Donne has sought to close the poem with a 'surprise'—a mere witty equivocation. A closer reading, however, suggests both intellectual consistency and a tough-minded realism: namely that the only love worth having is that which is also faithful.

Those poems usually dated to after 1600 are generally distinguished by a pervasive intellectual concentration, but it must be emphasised that it is often not that easy to group them chronologically. The dates given to them are approximations, commonly based upon internal evidence, such as the reference to 'Kings' in 'The Anniversary' which suggests a date sometime after James I's accession (1603), and these dates can often be called into question. In 'The Anniversary', for example, 'Kings' is modified by 'All', which implies a general rather than a specific application of the word; and similar objections can be made to the dating of 'The Sun Rising', which again, despite some internal evidence, seems to be pre-1600. Certainly, there is considerable stylistic variety between the various poems. In the case of 'The Anniversary' and 'The Sun Rising' both poems offer a self-sufficient world of love in contrast to the world of daily experience, but 'The Anniversary' depends less upon dramatic devices and witty inversions, deploying instead more serious forms of expression to illustrate the commonplace conflict of time with love, and the final emotional resolution is a celebration of physical life in the present as against a disembodied spiritual eternity:

> Here upon earth, we are kings, and none but we
> Can be such kings, nor of such subjects be . . .

By contrast, 'Air and Angels' exploits a conventional Petrarchan excuse and compliment to advance a different view of the relation between soul and body in love: in the poem the woman is flattered as a spiritual principle which must be given substance in a living body if it is to be loved. Here, Donne handles a difficult stanza form with great delicacy. The technique of inverting the normal word order, either for special emphasis or to facilitate rhyme, is obvious, particularly with the order of adverbial clauses and phrases. The conceits in lines 7 and 15–18 are formative. These, with the related analogies, the witty conclusion and the relation of scholastic theology to human love, epitomise the ingenuity of the Metaphysical style:

> Some lovely glorious nothing I did see,
>   But since my soul, whose child love is,
> Takes limbs of flesh, and else could nothing do,
>   More subtle than the parent is
> Love must not be, but take a body too . . .

Donne's consistent union of flesh and spirit sets a problem in the poem; namely that the excess of beauty renders 'love's pinnace over-fraught'. There is too much to love! Where does the poet begin, and how? Donne seeks to resolve this self-set problem by suggesting a new balance. He argues that if the woman will return his love, she will supply him with the only truly satisfying means, or 'sphere', for love—that is mutuality—a conclusion which recalls the subject of 'Love's Deity'. There is nothing very new here: both the subject and the images through which Donne explores it are commonplaces, but any reading of the poem impresses by the technical skill, the clarity and precision with which complex materials are handled.

Donne's use of the dramatic monologue, 'a dialogue of one' as he calls it in 'The Ecstasy' (line 74), his serious treatment of love and his emphasis upon the interdependence of body and soul are brilliantly demonstrated in the conjunction of erotic and religious elements in 'The Ecstasy'. The direct tradition behind the pastoral setting and lover's urging of his mistress in this poem is that of Sidney's Eighth Song in *Astrophil and Stella*; but the governing image of an ecstatic union of the lovers' souls is from the idea of religious ecstasy or spiritual union in which the soul 'leaves' the world of sense perception and communes with God. The poem can be divided into a threefold structure of setting, analysis and resolution. In the conceit of lines 7–8 Donne shows the souls of the lovers leaving their flesh and uniting through sight. The turning point is at line 50 where the flesh is celebrated for its power to enable the perception of the soul through the instruments of the senses. We realise that, instead of an ecstasy of sensual passion, we have witnessed a spiritual union which disciplines the flesh—'Small change, when we' are to bodies gone'—but does not decry it. As the following lines show, the libertine impulse has been mastered by spiritual idealism, and the body made the means of a transcendant vision:

As our blood labours to beget
　　Spirits, as like souls as it can,
Because such fingers need to knit
　　That subtle knot, which makes us man:

So must pure lovers' souls descend
　　T' affections, and to faculties,
Which sense may reach and apprehend,
　　Else a great prince in prison lies.

To our bodies turn we then, that so
　　Weak men on love revealed may look;
Love's mysteries in souls do grow,
　　But yet the body is his book.

Arguably one of Donne's finest poems, 'A Nocturnal Upon St

Lucy's Day, being the shortest day' demands quotation in full. It is uncertain who the recipient of the poem was (it may have been either Donne's patronness, Lucy Countess of Bedford, or Ann Donne herself); the poem's subject is anguish at the death of a beloved whom 'th' hydroptic earth hath drunk', and its imagery persistently expresses the attendant despair. Despite this emotional and personal undertow, the poem provides a considerable intellectual challenge as, in a typically Baroque manner, Donne draws upon a wide range of resources: leaping from one science to another, theological, astronomical, alchemical; moving from earth to heaven. Yet all this is woven into a unified argument.

The shortest day of the year provides the conceit, 'the year's midnight'; which sustains the controlling idea of the poem, namely the sense of inertia, nothingness, the experience of an absolute 'zero'. The first stanza has a contracting movement as Donne portrays a universe from which light and life are lost: sunlight dimmed to 'squibs'; the world itself on its deathbed, its essential life ('general balm') ebbing to 'the bed's feet'. This forceful conceit allows him to give a personal and dramatic direction to the poem:

> ... yet all these seem to laugh,
> Compared with me, who am their epitaph.

The body of the poem issues from that first stanza with its sense of universal contraction and final focus upon the poet. In the succeeding stanzas there is an 'expansion' as the poet makes himself a microcosm of the universe, and claims that he embodies a new paradox in nature, a quintessential nothingness. To follow the argument requires a careful and close reading, for Donne concentrates intellectual and emotional vigour both through the range of his references and through his ironic paradoxical associations—for example, the linking of 're-begot' (suggesting Christian spiritual regeneration) with such negative clusters as 'absence, darkness, death':

> 'Tis the year's midnight, and it is the day's,
> Lucy's, who scarce seven hours herself unmasks,
>   The sun is spent, and now his flasks
>   Send forth light squibs, no constant rays;
>   The world's whole sap is sunk:
> The general balm th' hydroptic earth hath drunk,
> Whither, as to the bed's-feet, life is shrunk,
> Dead and interred; yet all these seem to laugh,
> Compared with me, who am their epitaph.
>
> Study me then, you who shall lovers be
> At the next world, that is, at the next spring:

> For I am every dead thing,
> In whom love wrought new alchemy.
> For his art did express
> A quintessence even from nothingness,
> From dull privations, and lean emptiness
> He ruined me, and I am re-begot
> Of absence, darkness, death; things which are not.
>
> All others, from all things, draw all that's good,
> Life, soul, form, spirit, whence they being have;
> I, by love's limbeck, am the grave
> Of all, that's nothing, Oft a flood
> Have we two wept, and so
> Drowned the whole world, us two; oft did we grow
> To be two chaoses, when we did show
> Care to aught else; and often absences
> Withdrew our souls, and made us carcases.
>
> But I am by her death (which word wrongs her)
> Of the first nothing, the elixir grown;
> Were I a man, that I were one,
> I needs must know; I should prefer,
> If I were any beast,
> Some ends, some means; yea plants, yea stones detest,
> And love; all, all some properties invest;
> If I an ordinary nothing were,
> As shadow, a light, and body must be here.
>
> But I am none; nor will my sun renew.
> You lovers, for whose sake, the lesser sun
> At this time to the Goat is run
> To fetch new lust, and give it you,
> Enjoy your summer all;
> Since she enjoys her long night's festival,
> Let me prepare towards her, and let me call
> This hour her vigil, and her eve, since this
> Both the year's, and the day's deep midnight is.

From initial inertia the poem generates acute feeling and an emotional resolution. The tenor of the poem echoes the thought of Donne's religious poems. The speaker stands at an emotional turning-point: looking back with the instruments of memory and intellectual analysis in the body of the poem, and then forwards to spiritual fulfilment in the last four lines. In the last stanza his dead beloved becomes a spiritual light more powerful than the sun, and his love transcends the relative immaturity of the physical love associated with summer.

Epithalamia

Marriage songs or epithalamia (in Greek, *epithalamion* is a nuptial song) were a popular public genre introduced from Europe to England in the late sixteenth century. Spenser had provided a famous example which remains an obvious influence. The 'Epithalamion made at Lincoln's Inn' replaces spiritual and sensual rhetoric with farce, clever bawdiness and amiable satire, 'put forth, put forth that warm balm-breathing thigh'. Although the epithalamion for St Valentine's Day, written for the marriage of Princess Elizabeth to Frederick, the Elector Palatine, is a more formal public poem, the elements of humour are ineradicably laced with wit, and the traditional wedding-night humour handled with extraordinary taste. In these lines the ancient spherical notion of the universe supplies an amusingly elevated hyperbole to describe the progress of the bridegroom into his wife's bed:

> But now she is laid; what though she be?
> Yet there are more delays, for, where is he?
> He comes, and passes through sphere after sphere:
> First her sheets, then her arms, then any where,
> Let not this day, then, but this night be thine,
> Thy day was but the eve to this, O Valentine.

The *Anniversaries*

The *Anniversaries* belong to the period of Donne's life when he was hoping for court preferment and sought advancement through aristocrats such as Sir Robert Drury. An unusual feature of the two *Anniversaries* of 1611 and 1612 is that they are the only poems of Donne's that were published with his permission during his lifetime. Another is that they are commissioned pieces, sought by Sir Robert Drury to commemorate his daughter Elizabeth, whom Donne had never met. In *The Poetry of Meditation* Louis Martz has shown how meditative practices seem to have assisted the ordering of these poems into a sequence of meditations on a common theme.* Written in a manner sensitive to conventions—figurative speech, assumed humility—the *Anniversaries* display Donne's ability to make an otherwise formal task (in which his emotions were not directly involved) a powerful intellectual exercise, in which Elizabeth Drury is exalted from mere humanity to an ideal principle. In contrast with the steady decay of the world, she exhibits the kind of perfection that, according to the book of Genesis, mankind possessed in the Garden of Eden but which was forfeited after the Fall

* Louis Martz, *The Poetry of Meditation,* Yale University Press, New Haven, Connecticut, 1954, pp.219–48.

of Adam and Eve. This magnificent first *Anniversary*, 'An Anatomy of the World', is replete with formal expressions of despair at the world and life, and includes some famous lines such as those on the influence of the new philosophy (''Tis all in pieces, all coherence gone'), but emotional emphasis merges with intellectual analogy through Donne's insertion of key repetitions such as at lines 183–4:

> She, she is dead; she's dead: when thou know'st this,
> Thou know'st how poor a trifling thing man is.

In the second *Anniversary*, 'Of the Progress of the Soul', Donne's attention moves from the world to what lies beyond it and with more serious intent than in his youthful 'satire' *Metempsychosis* (despite those famous lines 'I launch at paradise'). The formal structure and approach are similar to the first *Anniversary*, and now Elizabeth Drury is made a pattern for the Christian in life and death. The subject matter here is familiar to Donne, and close reading discloses many echoes of the *Songs and Sonnets*, the sermons and *Devotions Upon Emergent Occasions*. Most impressive is the stark visual imagery used to relate body to soul, as in lines 9–17 and 293–7. In the first of these passages we are surprised by a brutal, but presumably familiar, analogy:

> Or as sometimes in a beheaded man,
> Though at those two red seas, which freely ran,
> One from the trunk, another from the head,
> His soul be sailed, to her eternal bed,
> His eyes will twinkle, and his tongue will roll,
> As though he beckoned, and called back his soul,
> He grasps his hands and he pulls up his feet,
> And seems to reach, and to step forth to meet
> His soul . . .

The effect of this is to express, dramatically and visually, the connection between body and soul, a concept radically advanced through the course of the poem. So, for example, at lines 293–7 Donne addresses the soul, and the intimacy of its connections with the body are reinforced by further graphic imagery:

> Thou look'st through spectacles; small things seem great
> Below; but up unto the watch-tower get,
> And see all things despoiled of fallacies:
> Thou shalt not peep through lattices of eyes,
> Nor hear through labyrinths of ears . . .

At the same time there is a sense of religious desperation in Donne: it is his own soul as well as Elizabeth Drury's with which he is concerned.

And so we can understand that the purpose of his strategies (for instance, in lines 339–57, 'Up, up, my drowsy soul . . . ') is to rouse his emotions to assist him as he summons his will to act. Such passages demonstrate yet again the remarkable sense of unity between flesh and spirit, heart and mind, which pervades Donne's poetry, and they also strongly suggest that the *Anniversaries* form a link between the secular and religious poetry as well as a link with some of the prose.

The *Divine Poems*

Introduction

Criticism of the *Divine Poems* has been dogged by Izaak Walton's *Life of Donne* which created the amiable fiction that Donne's secular poems were written before his ordination, and that his divine poems were the work of a sanctified spirit. In Walton's words, Donne was 'not so falne out with heavenly Poetry, as to forsake it, no not in his declining age, witnessed then by many divine Sonnets, and other high, holy, and harmonious composures'.* The work of Dame Helen Gardner in her edition of the *Divine Poems* has established the view that these poems generally belong to the middle period of Donne's life; those troubled years after marriage and before ordination, especially between 1607 and 1611, with only a few being written after ordination.

Dame Helen Gardner's dates locate these poems in the same context as Donne's polemical religious prose works *Pseudo-Martyr* (1610) and *Ignatius His Conclave* (1611) and the religious consciousness which underpins the *Anniversaries*, and this helps to explain the sense of tension which permeates the poems. With some notable exceptions the *Divine Poems* are not the work of a poet at peace with the world and his God, but one who, as in Satire 3, is still deciding his vocation and wondering how to express his faith.

The problem of religious poetry has always centred on the irreconcilable conflict between the ultimate claims of religious faith and the imaginative freedom of the poet. It is not necessary to share Donne's faith to enjoy these poems, though they may suggest what it is like to have or to seek that faith. In Dame Helen Gardner's words, 'No other religious poems make us feel so acutely the predicament of the natural man called to be the spiritual man.'† Thus, while a tradition of religious devotion and meditation lies behind them and influences their form and content, it is their dramatic and personal sense of engagement,

* Izaak Walton, *Life of Donne* (1640); quoted in Helen Gardner (ed.), *The Divine Poems of John Donne*, Clarendon Press, Oxford, 2nd edn, 1978, pp.xxxvii–viii.
† Helen Gardner (ed.), *The Divine Poems of John Donne*, p.xxxi.

their energy, passionate immediacy and the application of wit to an ultimately serious subject which gives them life for us.

La Corona

Although the sonnets of the *La Corona* sequence use Donne's dramatic 'I', they are the least personal of the *Divine Poems*. Their constant subject is the relationship between God and man, considered through a 'reformed' adaptation of a liturgical devotion—the Rosary—with its meditations upon the events of salvation history. As a form of devotion strongly associated with the Counter-Reformation, the Rosary was likely to offend some Protestant tastes, but its form provided an ordered sequence of major Christian mysteries and was a powerful aid to meditation. The fifteen Mysteries of the Rosary which provide raw material for Donne's poems are traditionally arranged in three groups: the Joyful Mysteries, which deal with the birth of Christ, and include the Annunciation, Visitation, Nativity, Presentation, Finding in the Temple; next, the Sorrowful Mysteries, which deal with the death of Christ—the Agony, Scourging, Crowning with Thorns, Bearing of the Cross, Crucifixion; finally, the Glorious Mysteries provide a series of subjects for meditation which deal with events after Christ's Resurrection; these include the Resurrection, Ascension, Coming of the Holy Ghost, Assumption, Coronation. Emphasis varies from one sonnet to another but generally reflects the influence of this form of vocal prayer rather than individual meditation. Although the theological approach in these poems is balanced it is also 'reformed' because Donne 'purges' the original devotional form of the Rosary to remove those details that were most objectionable to the reformed tastes, for instance such details as excessive verbal repetitions, too great an emphasis on the Virgin Mary, and those mysteries not based upon clear biblical authority.

Subject and technique explain the unusual unity that links the sequence. Subject, because the unity which links the devotional subjects is that drawn from the meditations of the Rosary itself. Technique, because first and last lines interlock between poems, their sestets alternate two rhyme schemes, and the last line of the final sonnet repeats the first line of the whole sequence. Again, as in a Rosary, the cycle of prayer is completed by a return to the beginning. By this formal interweaving Donne plaits a chaplet or wreath of sonnets so closely woven that no individual devotion or poem stands alone satisfactorily.

La Corona is less disturbing than Donne's *Holy Sonnets*; the language is assured, and the excesses of wit are so modified and controlled that the reader's appreciation of the sequence is never dominated by sheer intellectual or verbal force. Instead the context of vocal devotion dominates, and the commonplaces of faith and religious paradox are most respectfully handled. For example, Sonnet 2—on the Annunciation—provides Donne with an opportunity to exploit the human incongruity of the mystery wittily, but without the stark shock tactics typical of the *Holy Sonnets*:

> . . . yea thou art now
> Thy maker's maker, and thy father's mother,
> Thou hast light in dark; and shutt'st in little room,
> *Immensity cloistered in thy dear womb.*

On occasion Donne breathes new life into the formal vocal style of his Rosary materials by calling upon strategies which belong to the traditions of private devotion and meditation, and the way in which they encouraged the use of the imagination and emotions to contemplate and 'enter into' the subject of a meditation. So, for instance, in these poems Donne may directly place himself in the imagined scene, or address one of its participants. In the poem on the Finding in the Temple, Sonnet 4, he speaks to Joseph and draws our attention to the smallness of human knowledge in relation to its divine source, the God in human form, the youthful Christ:

> Joseph turn back; see where your child doth sit,
> Blowing, yea blowing out those sparks of wit,
> Which himself on the Doctors did bestow . . .

The personal emphasis which is typical of private meditation is clearly present in these poems. One telling example of this is Sonnet 6, on the Resurrection: here, Donne ingeniously adapts the devotion to concentrate upon his own resurrection rather than Christ's, and he exhibits the preoccupation with death that is characteristic of his Holy Sonnets.

> . . . nor shall to me
> Fear of first or last death, bring misery,
> If in thy little book my name thou enrol,
> Flesh in that long sleep is not putrefied,
> But made that there, of which, and for which 'twas;
> Nor can by any other means be glorified.

Holy Sonnets

Dating from 1609, earlier than *La Corona* and *A Litany*, the *Holy Sonnets* are distinctive in tone and technique. Of all Donne's religious poems the *Holy Sonnets* most sharply reveal his use of Ignatian meditational techniques (see above, pp.23–4), in their application of memory, composition of place, the emotions, and the movement through intellect and wonder to an internal debate, or colloquy, in which Divine mercy is sought. Twelve of the sonnets can be grouped as a sequence introduced by the poem 'As due by many titles I resign'; with six sonnets considering the 'Last Things'—death, heaven, hell and the Final Judgement, and six meditating upon various aspects of 'Divine Love'. Another four sonnets appear to be penitential, with three miscellaneous sonnets later in date—one of which deals with the death of Donne's wife.

The importance of the sonnet during the Renaissance is fundamental, and most Renaissance poets tried their hand at this verse form. The origins of the sonnet are usually attributed to thirteenth-century Italy, and sonnet sequences such as those famous sonnets of Dante to Beatrice, and Petrarch to Laura, established the form as a fitting and subtle instrument for the expression of intense feeling. In England, the example of Wyatt, Surrey (1517–47), Spenser and Shakespeare established its popularity amongst English poets, and variations were gradually made. The Italian form introduced by Wyatt (with some minor adaptations) followed the verse scheme that has been named after Petrarch: this was an eight-lined stanza (the octave) rhyming *abbaabba*, and a second stanza of six lines (the sestet) which usually rhymed *cdecde* or *cdcdcd*. Among the forms which developed in England was the version made popular by Spenser (which rhymed *abab bcbc cdcd ee*) and that named after Shakespeare (with its rhyme scheme of *abab cdcd efef gg*). The advantages of the sonnet form were its brevity and, most especially in the Petrarchan form which Donne so often used, the opportunity it offered for the octave to develop an idea which the sestet could then develop or 'turn' slightly. In short, the form of the sonnet lent itself to developing a 'crisis' in the octave, and then offering a 'resolution' to it in the sestet. Donne's *Holy Sonnets* and those by John Milton some years later, especially those few magnificent sonnets written after Milton's blindness, for example 'When I consider how my light is spent', are perhaps the most notable demonstrations in English literature of the use of the sonnet as a verse form for the exploration of a religious crisis.

The *Holy Sonnets* echo Donne's secular *Songs and Sonnets* in their ready application of wit to a sacred topic. This is manifest in their dramatic openings, their presentation of a poetic persona whose soul is striving for faith, their emotional and verbal violence, their intellectual strain and sometimes shocking imagery. The most impressive example of this is the sonnet 'Batter my heart, three-personed God', where Donne takes to an extreme the tradition of sexual imagery to describe the relation of the soul to God (the most telling example of this is the much debated Song of Solomon in the Bible) and demands God to overwhelm his disobedient soul as if in a rape. Implied in this violence is Donne's own humanity: his acute sense of his mortality and his desire for redemption.

The immediate appeal of these poems lies in their dramatic presentation of Donne's spiritual search. His extraordinarily successful deployment of familiar meditative techniques suggests he found them congenial to his personality and poetic talents. 'At the round earth's imagined corners', a meditation upon one of the Last Things, is representative:

> At the round earth's imagined corners, blow
> Your trumpets, angels, and arise, arise
> From death, you numberless infinities
> Of souls, and to your scattered bodies go,
> All whom the flood did, and fire shall o'erthrow,
> All whom war, dearth, age, agues, tyrannies,
> Despair, law, chance, hath slain, and you whose eyes,
> Shall behold God, and never taste death's woe.
> But let them sleep, Lord, and me mourn a space,
> For, if above all these, my sins abound,
> 'Tis late to ask abundance of thy grace,
> When we are there; here on this lowly ground,
> Teach me how to repent; for that's as good
> As if thou hadst sealed my pardon, with thy blood.

In the octave Donne uses the 'composition of place' to give imaginative substance to the concept of the Last Judgement. As if regarding a map (a favourite image of his), he condenses space and time, while with enormous verbal energy—as in the repetitions, actual or implied, of 'arise' and 'numberless infinities'—and direct address, he 'paints' the scene. What the octave visualises, the sestet applies. Against the cosmic sweep of the octave, the sestet juxtaposes the poet's personal and direct address to God. The two contexts are condensed in the pithy juxtaposition in line 12 of 'there/here'. A touch, witty and pertinent, but typical of Donne, is the final plea that divine initiative make good human frailty— 'Teach me how to repent'.

Occasional poems

A Litany

As with *La Corona*, *A Litany* is another adaptation from a form of devotion associated with the liturgy or general vocal devotions of the Church; in this instance the form is that of a penitential prayer in which the clergy lead petitions and the congregation make responses. Usually dated to about 1608, that this poem precedes his ordination is clear from a letter, written during a time of sickness when Donne was considering his views on Roman Catholicism in such prose works as *Biathanatos* and *Pseudo-Martyr*, in which he mentions a 'meditation in verse, which I call a Litany' and excuses himself 'as a lay man' for taking 'such divine and public names, to his own little thoughts'. One particular reference to his Roman Catholic tradition, and his move away from it, is his allusion to the martyrs in stanza 10—'for oh, to some / Not to be martyrs, is a martyrdom.'

From this Catholic devotion with its invocations of the Virgin Mary and the saints, Donne fashions a concise expression of the Anglican *via media*, by which Anglicans have generally meant the path of moderation that their Church has steered between the essentials of Catholic tradition and the insights of the Protestant reformers. As Dame Helen Gardner remarks, 'in many ways it is the most Anglican of the Divine Poems':* while devotion to Virgin and saints remains, Donne conforms to the Anglican Articles of Faith by making the address to God.

Liturgical objectivity, even impersonality, presents potential problems for the poet using the liturgy as a model, but Donne overcomes this by adroit variation of the liturgical use of personal pronouns, switching from the plural 'Us' or 'We' to 'I' or 'Me' as his focus shifts to a personal relationship. The effect is to internalise and dramatise the object of his meditation. We see this, for instance, in the meditation addressed to Christ where meditative technique fuses with conceit:

O be thou nail'd unto my heart,
And crucified again . . .

'The Cross'

Since Christ embraced the Cross itself, dare I
His image, th' image of his Cross deny?

The style of this poem shows it to be an early one, being more a verse letter than one of the *Divine Poems* proper. These opening lines indicate the historical context which dates the poem, James I's Hampton Court Conference of 1603 and the Puritan Millenary Petition which included a demand for abolition of the sign of the cross at baptism.

While the conference reminded the Puritans that the cross as an ecclesiastical ornament was rare, Donne defends it as a personal object of devotion against prejudices—'misgrounded law'. By his ingenious accumulation of diverse verbal or visual usages of the cross—whether in maps, ships' spars or the human anatomy—he not only wittily puns upon several senses of 'cross' but grounds the image of the cross in the

* Helen Gardner (ed.), *The Divine Poems of John Donne*, p.xxvi.

natural and divine order of the cosmos. As his argument concludes, 'Be covetous of crosses, let none fall.'

'Resurrection, imperfect'

This poem is incomplete—'imperfect' as the final tag suggests (*Desunt cætera*— the remainder is lacking). Its dominant conceit—that the grave is the limbeck* which refines purer elements from baser—is derived from alchemy, the so-called 'secret art' which was concerned with esoteric ambitions such as the transformation of baser metals into gold and the discovery of the elixir of life. The same image recurs in the 'Elegy on Lady Markham' of about the same date, and displays Donne's capacity for giving the most conventional, and even stale, religious images new life. Here Christ manifests the connection between spirit and flesh, and is the power 'to make even sinful flesh like his'.

'Upon the Annunciation and Passion falling upon one day. 1608'

The occasion of this poem is indicated by the title: in 1608 the Feast of the Annunciation (25 March), on which day the Church remembers the conception by the Virgin Mary of the Christ child, coincided with Good Friday, the day on which the Church remembers his death. This paradoxical conjunction of birth and death prompted a witty meditation with many analogies that recur in Donne's later poems and sermons. Upon this paradox Donne lays the foundation for the various conceits of the poem, and his delight in it demonstrates his shaping imagination, his passion for concentricity—'of them both a circle emblem is', or, 'As in plain maps, the furthest west is east'. Throughout the poem the central idea is developed in a form similar to an Ignatian meditation: the composition of place, 'today'; the application of memory, 'she sees at once the Virgin Mother . . .'; the use of understanding by Donne's reference to the custom of the Church, and, finally, the personal application in the concluding colloquy:

> This treasure then, in gross, my soul uplay,
> And in my life retail it every day.

'Good Friday, 1613. Riding Westward'

We can fix a date for this poem from a journey Donne made on Good Friday, 2 April 1613 between the home of Sir Henry Goodyer and that of Sir Edward Herbert, and he appears to have composed it *en route*. The formal arrangement reflects the manner in which meditative tech-

---

* Limbeck as a rule means to distil, to treat as in an alembic; as a noun it is an archaic form of alembic, an apparatus used in distilling, a gourd-shaped vessel with a cap (the alembic proper), the beak of which conveys the product of distillation to a vessel called a receiver.

niques provided a framework for a poem of this sort, while the conceits and verbal play mark Donne's fusion of wit and spiritual seriousness.

Structurally, the poem is simple and accomplished. Through the first ten lines the conceit of man's soul as a sphere marks a 'composition' of the occasion which initiates and sustains a meditation. Following the precepts of medieval astronomy, Donne compares the universe, where the spherical movements determined by angelic intelligences could be disturbed by 'foreign motions' or external forces, to the soul where the obligations of devotion are diverted by various aspects of human necessity, 'pleasure or business'. From lines 11 to 13 Donne, though absent from the religious observance of the day, imaginatively re-creates and meditates upon it. The immediate link is the contradiction of the direction symbolism. For it is in the east that Christ died, while Donne rides west, yet it is also in the east that the sun rises, and that, in its turn, is an image of the Resurrection:

> . . . I am carried towards the west
> This day, when my soul's form bends toward the east.

The accretion of contrasts and paradoxes—visual, verbal and conceptual—dramatically enforces the substance of the meditation and lead to his personal application of its realisations through his direct address to God in the colloquy which closes the poem in lines 36–42:

> O Saviour, as thou hang'st upon the tree;
> I turn my back to thee, but to receive
> Corrections . . .
> Restore thine image, so much, by thy grace,
> That thou mayst know me, and I'll turn my face.

While here Donne's 'reversal' makes an excuse—more witty than convincing—for his westward journeying, the poem remains a fine example of his capacity to endue an immediate occasion with unexpected moral significance.

'To Mr. Tilman after he had taken orders'
The ordination of Mr Tilman in December 1618 provides a base-date for this slight demonstration of Donne's epistolary style. The warm tone and focus of the poem reflect Donne's deep concerns: he defends the priestly vocation against the low regard in which it was held by the nobility—a somewhat ironic stance since such a consideration may have delayed Donne's own entry into orders.* A characteristic touch is his transformation of human ambition:

> What function is so noble, as to be
> Ambassador to God and destiny?

* See Helen Gardner (ed.), *The Divine Poems of John Donne*, pp.127–32.

'Upon the Translation of the Psalms'
This poem with its allusion to the Sidneys' influential translations of the
Psalms displays Donne's strong lines, intellectual urgency and recurring
images; for example, God as a circle and the human soul as a musical
instrument to be tuned (lines 29–30), an image which is developed in
'Hymn to God my God, in my Sickness'. Addressed to God the poem
transcends literary compliment to become an act of vocal prayer.

Hymns

'A Hymn to Christ, at the Author's last going into Germany'
Written relatively late in his life, and in contrast to the meditative poem
which may be dramatic or introspective as Donne chooses, the *Hymns*
are direct vocal prayers to God which confront death and judgement. 'A
Hymn to Christ, at the Author's last going into Germany' was written to
mark Donne's departure with the Earl of Doncaster's diplomatic
mission from May 1619 to January 1620 and the serious preparation for
death which such a hazardous sea-journey involved. From the opening
stanza with its emblematic visual imagery, Donne moves quickly in the
next three stanzas to more abstract speculations and makes the
immediate journey an image for renunciation of the world and for the
final journey, death itself. Though the sombre rhythms are reminiscent
of Lutheran hymns, the thrust of the thought, imagery and language is
toward an affirmation of confidence in the abiding love of God:

> To see God only, I go out of sight:
>   And to 'scape stormy days, I choose
>   An everlasting night.

'Hymn to God my God, in my Sickness'
Usually dated, with 'A Hymn to God the Father', to Donne's serious
illness during 1623, this poem demonstrates Donne's consistent and
witty use of vigorous, punning language and eclectic imagery—music,
medicine, geography, religion—in a devotional meditation which engages the prospect of imminent death and the goal of the heavenly
paradise which can only be reached through Calvary. The concentricity
of Donne's thought is, paradoxically, the means of his 'progression' in
faith as his thought circles the nature of God:

> We think that Paradise and Calvary,
>   Christ's Cross, and Adam's tree, stood in one place;
> Look Lord, and find both Adams met in me . . .

'A Hymn to God the Father
While similar to other *Hymns* in its wit, personal address and subject,

this poem is lyrical rather than meditative, and indeed, was set to music several times during the seventeenth century. The control over language and technique is assured. The well-known pun upon the poet's name is a poignant touch but is also an organising principle for the whole poem as the repetitions in the refrain prepare us for its dramatic, personal closure. This shows how the least pretentious of the devices of wit could be turned into a pivot for urgent thought—and not mere display. Through its dramatic tension between the refrain 'thou hast not done', which is the foil for the triumphant conclusion (echoing the last words on the cross) 'thou has done', the poem is a moving display of Donne's intellectual and imaginative agility.

The prose works

General features

Donne's prose works range from minor studies to occasional pieces of more significance, and demonstrate, as does his poetry, a reaction against an earlier literary fashion. Between 1608 and 1614 he produced a series of prose works of considerable intellectual and stylistic maturity which are of particular interest as they show his progress toward religious faith; while between 1615 and 1630 he delivered about one hundred and sixty sermons of polished and persuasive power. His witty antithetical style suggests the influence of Senecan models rather than the elegant simplicity of Cicero, while conceits, puns, wit and intellect are characteristic.

Miscellaneous works

An early collection of pieces, *Paradoxes and Problems* demonstrates Donne's satirical skill in the trivial rhetorical exercises typical of this Renaissance genre with its debate upon such topics as 'A Defence of Womens Inconstancy'. The work also displays the witty convolutions of thought that the *Songs and Sonnets* achieve.

Biathanatos (1607/8) is more than a scholastic apology for suicide; in many respects Donne's 'defence' is a satire on the specious and often over-subtle reasoning that philosophers and theologians frequently applied to moral issues. Stylistically, the capitalised nouns, the habitual aphorisms, the frequent use of analogies and the general rhetorical approach are typical. Its aphoristic, argumentative prose and its intellectual mix of diverse philosophical traditions (for instance both the Stoic philosophy of endurance and its opposite, the pursuit of pleasure associated with Epicureanism, can be found together with Christian scepticism) on the one hand further illustrate the talent for analogy revealed in Donne's poetry, and, on the other, are eloquent demonstrations of his ability to balance the claims of natural law, ecclesiastical authority and reason. His witty relativisation of the 'lights' of both nature and reason, these being, together with the Bible, fundamental sources of authority to which the thinker could appeal, echoes his satires of the 1590s, in particularly Satire 3 with its scepticism about any ultimacy in human institutions and claims. For example:

> But because of these two kinds of light, the first is too weake, and the other false, (for onely colour is the object of sight, and we trust not candlelight to discerne Colours) we have therefore the Sunne, which is the Fountaine and Treasure of all created light, for an Embleme of that third best light of our understanding, which is the Word of God.*

Longest of his prose works, *Pseudo-Martyr* (1610) emphasises Donne's moderation and his shift from his family's Catholic tradition. Aimed at the Catholic recusants who opposed the Oath of Allegiance enforced by James I after the Gunpowder Plot (1605), it criticises those aspiring to become martyrs on moral and legal grounds. The same year, *Ignatius His Conclave* answered Cardinal Bellarmine's (1542–1621) attack upon the Oath of Supremacy and Allegiance with a light-hearted Menippean satire (so named for the gentle indictments of folly made by Menippus of Gadara (300BC)) on the vanity of the Jesuits. Enacted before Lucifer, Donne's debate in hell between Ignatius, Copernicus, Columbus (c.1445–1506) and Machiavelli addresses a serious theological problem while wittily considering contemporary ideas. This theological concern is more formally developed in Donne's next prose work, the *Essays in Divinity* (?1611), where, clearly influenced by Augustine's mix of philosophical meditation, prayer and scriptural exegesis, he comments upon Genesis and Exodus—a study which is reflected in the themes of the *Anniversaries*.

Devotions Upon Emergent Occasions (1624)

'Emergent' means 'urgent', and Donne's serious illness of 1623 produced two hymns and this highly regarded prose work full of passion, wit, intense imagery and learning. It is divided into twenty-three sections, each further subdivided into a meditation upon the human condition. Employing visual, concrete terms that recall Ignatian technique, and containing a dramatic 'expostulation' with

* *Biathanatos*, 1646, Third Part, Distinction 1, Section 1, p.153. Quoted in A.C. Partridge, *John Donne: Language and Style*, André Deutsch, London, 1978, p.158.

God along with prayers of contrition and thanksgiving, these devotions provide a grotesque depiction of Donne's illness and his introspective, dramatic nature. The technique of the sermon joins with that of meditation, rhetoric with metaphysical imagery, the particular suggests the universal, as the bells of the neighbouring Church of St Gregory provoke this imagery of Donne's frequently quoted Meditation 17:

> No man is an *Iland*, intire of it selfe; every man is a peece of the *Continent*, a part of the *maine*, if a *Clod* bee washed away by the Sea, *Europe* is the lesse, as well as if a *Promontorie* were, as well as if a *Mannor* of thy *friends* or of *thine owne* were; any mans *death* diminishes *me*, because I am involved in *Mankinde*, And therefore never send to know for whom the *bell* tolls; It tolls for *thee*.

Sermons

Donne was the most famous preacher of his time, and in their Augustinian oscillation between meditation, expostulation and prayer, his sermons recall the prose style of the *Devotions Upon Emergent Occasions*, while their meticulous organisation marks a strong sense of preaching as an art. These works reflect the essentials of his mature prose style and place him alongside other masters of prose such as Thomas Browne, Jeremy Taylor and John Milton. They display a varying style based upon judicious use of short sentences, balanced antithesis and asymetrical construction with the marshalling of one subordinate clause upon another, all leading towards a final dramatic climax. So finely is this done, that in many instances passages cannot be shortened without losing their cumulative effect.

Wit and learning are never absent here. On the one hand, the range of learning is impressive: the sermons are filled with allusions to astronomy, mathematics, medicine, geography and natural history. In addition, Donne exhibits his expertise in theology—both Catholic and Reformed—and moves easily through the different traditions and sources of authority. On the other hand, much of the force of the sermons is derived from Donne's ingenious analogies which explain the spiritual through the physical and apply it to individual experience. The effect is of continual elaboration, as a dominant idea is circled and recircled and all its connotations are explored. For instance, the image of the circle or sphere, so recurrent in Donne's thought in both prose and poetry, suggests something of his style:

> ... Our grave is upward, and our heart is upon Jacob's ladder, in the way, and nearer to heaven. Our daily Funerals are some Emblemes of that; for though we be laid down in the earth after, yet

we are lifted up upon mens shoulders before. We rise in the descent to death, and so we do in the descent to the contemplation of it. In all the Potters house, is there one vessell made of better stuffe then clay? There is his matter. And of all formes, a Circle is the perfectest, and art thou loath to make up that Circle, with returning to the earth again?*

While this use of paradox is typical of Metaphysical wit and is characteristic of Donne's sermons, the passage also reflects his innate sense of order. This same idea and visual image are further elaborated in another sermon:

If you looke upon this world in a Map, you find two Hemispheres, two half worlds. If you crush Heaven into a Map, you may find two Hemisphears too, two half heavens; Halfe will be Joy, and halfe Glory; for in these two, the joy of heaven, and the glory of heaven, is all heaven often represented unto us. And as of those two Hemisphears of the world, the first hath been knowne long before, but the other, (that of America, which is the richer in treasure) God reserved for later Discoveries; so though he reserve that Hemisphear of heaven, which is the Glory thereof, to the Resurrection, yet the other Hemisphear, the Joy of Heaven, God opens to our Discovery, and delivers for our habitation even whilst we dwell in this world. As God hath cast upon the unrepentant sinner two deaths, a temporall, and a spirituall death, so hath he breathed into us two lives.†

In the one, Donne uses the circle to resign mankind to mortality; in the other, to provide incongruous analogies which tease the mind but foster acceptance of divine providence.

Much of the contemporary appeal of the sermons is attributable to Donne himself. They were delivered with a sense of dramatic performance which, though the very opposite of being artificial, meant nonetheless that the sermons were 'enacted'. In his *Life of Donne*, Walton refers to Donne's pulpit manner and tells how he 'preached the Word so, as showed his own heart was possest with those very thoughts and joys that he laboured to distill into others: A Preacher in earnest; weeping sometimes for his Auditory, sometimes with them . . . and all this with a particular grace and an unexpressible addition of comeliness.' One passage from the sermons may serve to illustrate the vigorous style, sharp wit, honesty and self-criticism which attracted his congregations:

* Quoted in Evelyn M. Simpson and George R. Potter, *The Sermons of John Donne*, 10 vols, University of California Press, Berkeley and Los Angeles, 1984, Vol. IV, p.51.
† Quoted in Evelyn M. Simpson and George R. Potter, *The Sermons of John Donne*, Vol. VII, p.69.

I throw my selfe down in my Chamber, and I call in, and invite God, and his Angels thither, and when they are there, I neglect God and his Angels, for the noise of a Flie, for the ratling of a Coach, for the whining of a doore; I talke on, in the same posture of praying; Eyes lifted up; knees bowed downe; as though I prayed to God; and, if God, or his Angels should aske me, when I last thought of God in that prayer, I cannot tell: Sometimes I finde that I had forgot what I was about, but when I began to forget it, I cannot tell. A memory of yesterdays pleasures, a fear of to morrows dangers, a straw under my knee, a noise in mine eare, a light in mine eye, an anything, a nothing, a fancy, a Chimera in my braine, troubles me in my prayer. So certainly is there nothing, nothing in spirituall things, perfect in this world.*

* *LXXX Sermons*, No.80, p.820. Quoted by Evelyn M. Simpson in 'The Literary Value of Donne's Sermons' (Section IV of the General Introduction to *The Sermons of John Donne*, Vol. 1), and reproduced in Helen Gardner (ed.), *John Donne: A Collection of Critical Essays*, Prentice-Hall, Engelwood Cliffs, New Jersey, 1962, p.144.

Chapter 4

The school of Donne

A style and influence

Here lies a King, that rul'd as hee thought fit
The universall Monarchy of wit

Follower of Jonson though he was, Carew, in his concluding lines to
his elegy in praise of Donne, testifies to Donne's capacity to excite both
admiration and emulation from his fellow poets. His example also
reminds us how fluid the boundaries were between the various poetic
styles, and also to what extent we are justified in referring to a 'school
of Donne'. If there is any truth in the idea of a 'school', it lies in the
fact that Donne demonstrated a way of thinking and writing that had
an appeal in a society that remained unsettled until the Restoration. It
must be remembered, too, that the poets of this society formed, in
many respects, a small and charmed elite: Donne was a wit—a man of
intellect—writing for other wits. The heart of his circle seems likely to
have been established when most of his poetry was written, while he
was still in his twenties: first at Oxford* and then at Lincoln's Inn
which he entered in 1592, and the dedications to various poems give us
a fair idea of what this circle had in common. Nearly all of its members
came from among the wealthy or landed middle classes. They had been
to the universities and Inns of Court, had entered the respected professions or Court, and—perhaps most relevant—either wrote poetry or at
least were clearly regarded as men of wit. The essence of the school is
the poets' intimacy, their amateur status as poets, and their common
privileged background and cultivated taste. We can gain some idea of
the intimacy of the circle from the way in which Donne's *Biathanatos*
was circulated: Donne sent the work to Sir Robert Ker with a letter in
which he remarks that 'no hand hath passed upon it to copy it, nor
many eyes to read it: only to some particular friends in both Universities, then when I writ it, I did communicate it'.† Presumably, many
of the poems were passed around in the same way.

* See A. Alvarez. *The School of Donne*, Chatto & Windus, London, 1970, Appendix 1,
pp.187–95.
† From *Letters to Severall Persons of Honour*, 1651, p. 19. Quoted in A. Alvarez, *The
School of Donne*, p.35.

The influence of Donne's work can be seen most clearly in later poets such as Herbert, Crashaw and Marvell. In the interim, his circle of friends generally wrote in the conventional Elizabethan manner and only occasionally produced poems which emulated both his learned, dialectical, highly epigrammatic style and his argumentative, colloquial, harsh tone. It is important to note, then, that although the 'school of Donne' includes major talents, its members seem to have been both varied and a generation younger than Donne himself.

The circle

Donne defined an intellectual tone which appealed to the taste of young middle-class intellectuals who were to enter the professions. The further the 'followers' were from Donne himself, the less was their adherence to his essential intellectual rigour and personally engaged tone, and the greater their emulation of what could so easily be mere technique. Later developments of his style were to reflect the milieus of Court, Church and University as the influence of his literary innovations spread to a wider audience.

The style of writers such as Lovelace and Carew only superficially resembled that of Donne, and in this token resemblance they reflected the Caroline courtly style of wit that evolved from him but which lacked his personal engagement. Their dramatic openings and occasional metrical harshness strike an attitude, a mere formality, and anticipate the easy social graces which characterise the Augustan taste of eighteenth-century writers such as Addison (1672–1719) and Pope (1688–1744), both of whom greatly valued and eloquently expressed the qualities of order, symmetry, decorum and refined sensibility.

On the other hand the epigrammatic extremes of such university wits as Austin (1613–69), Hall and Cleveland discredited both the Metaphysical style and Donne's endeavours. Severe critics included Dryden and—most crushingly—Dr Johnson, who said of these poets that all their poetry was aimed 'to show their learning'. The criticism is apt, because Cleveland in particular demonstrates how the technical vocabulary of scholarship could be used without the imaginative coherence and control of Donne. In Cleveland's hands the concentrated energy of the best Metaphysicals, and their exhilarating rejuvenation of such forms of figurative language as the conceit, dwindle to a device for display. They become a linguistic trick for scoring effects, a matter of associations of sight and sound without the substance and rigour which characterises, for instance, Donne's far-ranging grasp of disparate materials.

Sir Henry Wotton (1568–1639)

Wotton was contemporary with Donne and formed a lasting friendship with him from their days at Oxford and the Inns of Court. He was with Donne on Essex's expeditions to Cadiz (1596) and the Azores (1597). A poet with several good poems to his credit in *Reliquiae Wottonianae* (1651), he was Ambassador to Venice and went on to become Provost at Eton. He would have written Donne's biography, but died before he could do so; the task was taken over by Izaak Walton who, moreover, wrote a life of Wotton as well (1670).

The poems for which Wotton is remembered demonstrate his intellectual and cultural accomplishments. They include the Horatian 'Character of a Happy Life', the witty, amorous 'On a Bench as I sate a Fishing', and the cultivated 'You Meaner Beauties of the Night' with its logically developed and carefully expressed contrasts. The conclusion to this last poem is carefully poised; its compliment to the daughter of James I, the Queen of Bohemia on whose behalf Wotton had been employed, is founded upon carefully established intellectual and moral premises. It can be compared with Donne's *Anniversaries* to show how, despite the striking differences of subject and tone, intellectual clarity dominates:

So when my *Mistres* shal be *seene*
  In *form* and *Beauty* of her mind,
By *Vertue* first, then *Choyce*, a *Queen,*
  Tell me, if *she* were not design'd
Th' *Eclypse* and *Glory* of her kind?

Edward, Lord Herbert of Cherbury (1583–1648)

The Herbert family was particularly influenced by Donne's personality and poetry. Both of Magdalen Herbert's sons knew Donne well, and through them was spun a network of associations which carried Donne's influence well beyond his lifetime. Through George Herbert's example poets such as Vaughan and Crashaw found the attraction of Donne's style and eventually became associated with the Metaphysical school. There were further associations of a minor and more intimate kind. For example, Edward Lord Herbert of Cherbury took Aurelian Townshend with him to France (1608–9), and later used Carew —a friend of such Cavalier poets as Suckling, Davenant and Godolphin— as his secretary, and all three exchanged verses. His autobiography records his adventures and vividly presents him as that mix of idealist and realist, hero and sceptic, which reflects the social flux of his time.

Edward, Lord Herbert of Cherbury, is close to Donne in style as he is in age but he is not a particularly original poet. He lacks Donne's realism and intellectual urgency, though his speculative approach shows Donne's influence, and he shares Donne's tight structure and dialectical interest—a notable consequence of this being that his poems are often instruments for an inner debate. However, the much quoted poem 'An Ode upon a Question moved, whether Love should continue for ever?' registers very clearly his distinction from Donne. Here his philosophical interest in truth is made specific by a dramatic setting, but the scene lacks concreteness, its diction is simpler, its interest more philosophic. It is what one would expect from the author of *De Veritate* (1624), a work which laid the foundation for English Deism, or 'natural religion', with its attempt to develop belief in a 'God' without the supernaturalism associated with Christianity. In this context the final lines of 'An Ode upon a Question moved' are particularly revealing:

This said, in her up-lifted face,
　Her eyes which did that beauty crown,
　Were like two starres, that having faln down,
Look up again to find their place:

While such a moveless silent peace
　Did seize on their becalmed sense,
　One would have thought some influence
Their ravish'd spirits did possess.*

The effect of the poem hinges on familiarity with Platonism, which was particularly influential during the Renaissance. As elaborated upon by numerous scholars, the essentials of this philosophy were based on the doctrine of 'two worlds': on the one hand, a changeless spiritual world of ideal forms; on the other, its imperfect copy, a finite world of flux. This fundamental concept generated such powerful images as the idea that the body was the prison of the soul, and the idea of 'platonic love' which taught that physical beauty was a poor reflection of the eternal beauty to which the lover should aspire.

Lord Herbert of Cherbury's emphasis on Platonism marks a clear distinction between his style and Donne's. Whereas in Donne's works philosophy is exploited to serve poetic and human ends, here Lord Herbert of Cherbury's poem is merely an excuse for philosophising. In fact, when he writes about love, he is closer in spirit to the Italian Neo-platonists, scholars such as Castiglione (1467 – 1529) and Pico della Mirandola (1463–94) who adapted Platonic thought and attempted a fusion of various philosophical elements from the Jewish Cabala,

---

* Lines 133–40. Quoted in H.J.C. Grierson, *Metaphysical Lyrics and Poems of the Seventeenth Century*, Clarendon Press, Oxford, 1921, reprinted 1972, p.33.

Christian theology, as well as the philosophy of Plato and Aristotle. Such poems as this, and also 'The Idea' and 'Platonic Love', are—when compared with Donne's 'The Ecstasy'—markedly less realistic, less able to engage with the realities of the flesh.

Aurelian Townshend (1583–?1643)

Little is known of Townshend, though he was well known as a writer of court masques and collaborated in their production with the architect and designer Inigo Jones (1573–1652). Author of no book or collection of verse, though represented in various miscellanies, Townshend remains a shadowy figure on the fringe of the circle of Donne's influence.

What distinguishes Townshend is his flash of brilliance, his capacity to be unique, though this is only caught in a few poems. Though his style is Elizabethan, his way of thinking reflects Donne: at his best he achieves a lyric grace which is sustained by intellectual seriousness. The formal and musical effects of some of his poems suggest his involvement in the masques that were so popular during this period. Over all there plays a cool intelligence which anticipates Marvell: for example, the intensely stylised 'Dialogue betwixt Time and a Pilgrime' where elegance and intellect combine:

> If thou art Time, these Flow'rs have Lives,
>   And then I fear,
> Under some Lilly she I love
>   May now be growing there.*

Henry King (1592–1669)

A contemporary of George Herbert and a friend of Donne, King is a master of epigrammatical wit, emphatic and ingenious strong lines with unpredictable pauses and varied lengths. In contrast to the poise of the Cavalier poets, his fondness for the conventions of Petrarchan praise looks back to the traditions of Elizabethan verse, while his incisiveness and wit show the influence of Donne. His most admired poem, 'An Exequy', which was written in 1624, laments the death of his wife, and recalls Donne's own anguish at the death of Ann More in the Holy Sonnet 'Since she whom I lov'd'. Here King is stricken, as was Donne, by the violence of time and the frailty of human life, yet manages to treat complex and profound emotions with exceptional wit and intellectual control. The final lines are a superb instance of his

* Quoted in Helen Gardner (ed.), *The Metaphysical Poets*, Penguin Books, Harmondsworth, 1966.

fusion of enduring human affection and physical experience with
devout anticipation of a reunion beyond the grave:

> 'Tis true, with shame and grief I yield,
> Thou like the van first took'st the field,
> And gotten hath the victory
> In thus adventuring to die
> Before me, whose more years might crave
> A just precedence in the grave.
> But hark! my pulse like a soft drum
> Beats my approach, tells thee I come;
> And slow howe'er my marches be,
> I shall at last sit down by thee.
> The thought of this bids me go on,
> And wait my dissolution
> With hope and comfort. Dear, forgive
> The crime, I am content to live
> Divided, with but half a heart,
> Till we shall meet and never part.*

* Quoted in T.G.S. Cain (ed.), *Jacobean and Caroline Poetry. An Anthology*, Methuen,
London, 1981, pp.243–4.

Chapter 5

George Herbert

Life

> [My] meaning . . . is in these Sonnets, to declare my resolution to be,
> that my poor Abilities in *Poetry*, shall be all, and ever consecrated to
> God's glory.*

These casual, perhaps excessively self-conscious, remarks indicate
some elements that are central to the personality and writing of George
Herbert (1593–1633); in particular his sense of his own talents and his
sense of dedication. Herbert's view of himself explains—and is borne
out by—the various accounts of his saintly life as rector in the parish of
Bemerton. One scholar has pointed out that the tradition of Herbert's
piety is not simply due to the excessive generosity of Izaak Walton. As
he remarks:

> Herbert's complete devotion to his calling, once he had accepted it,
> and his fitness for it, are evident, not only from the stories which
> Walton collected . . . but from earlier and more trustworthy testi-
> mony. 'Holy Mr. Herbert' is no invention of Izaak Walton, writing
> thirty-seven years after his death and without first-hand knowledge
> ('I have only seen him'), but it is a contemporary estimate.†

While much of Herbert's earnestness can be accounted for by the religious temperament of the age, much is also due to his family
background. Born into a family with a tradition of noble and talented
service, it was natural for him to aspire to a career at Court, for he
possessed the background for high expectations of employment in
public affairs. Fortunately Herbert possessed the grace of manner and
the intellectual accomplishments that would help him to achieve such a
position. To realise his ambitions he used his family's influence to
assist him to secure the position of Orator to Cambridge University in

---

* Part of a letter from Herbert to his mother, New Year, 1609/10. Quoted in F.E.
Hutchinson (ed.), *The Works of George Herbert*, Clarendon Press, Oxford, 1948,
reprinted 1971, p.363. Unless otherwise indicated, all quotations from Herbert's works
are taken from this edition.
† F.E. Hutchinson (ed.), *The Works of George Herbert*, p.xxxvi.

January 1619/20, a position he held for seven years, and which had been used by its previous incumbents as a means to high secular office. This aristocratic background figures in his poetry through his unostentatious references to music, science and scholarship, and his general assurance of expression and implied intimacy with a variety of social contexts. Ambition in such a position is understandable: indeed Walton records that Herbert in his early years 'put too great a value on his parts [abilities] and parentage.'* In the light of such a considered judgement, Herbert's decision to enter the Church, soon after the death of King James I in 1625, is all the more surprising. For, while his ordination did not compel him to stay in the parish ministry, it effectively disqualified him from secular employment.

Though what provoked the change remains obscure—whether the death of influential patrons, self-distrust in his own talents, or some profound religious experience – the consequences were profound for Herbert's poetry. The sense of tension between a courtly public role where his considerable talents could flourish, and his far more restricted private life as a parish clergyman, provides a distinctive tone for the poems. Certainly this tension surfaces in a poem such as the well-known 'The Collar', but, more subtly, it also lies behind the mature considered acceptance of 'The Pearl' with its contrast between the rich fulfilment of sensual being and the demands of his religious commitment. That these poems are to be understood as an intimate account of a spiritual struggle is clear from the description Herbert gave of them in his last note to Nicolas Ferrar when he stated that Ferrar would find in them 'a picture of the many spiritual Conflicts that have past betwixt God and my Soul, before I could subject mine to the will of Jesus my Master, in whose service I have now found perfect freedom.'†

A distinctive style

Until recently Herbert's status as a poet rested mainly upon his association with Donne and the Metaphysical style. But for many critics, his lack of Donne's witty detachment, and, above all, his exclusively religious subject matter, counted against his being seriously considered as a major poet in his own right. Donne has generally been more favourably received by modern readers who have admired the dramatic tension and vigour of his writing, while Herbert's achievement of a subtle aesthetic and emotional order in poetry has unfortunately won less immediate acceptance as a mark of literary excellence. Yet Herbert's work consistently shows how a finely achieved 'wholeness' can exist without Donne's sharply fragmented structure. It is only as

* Quoted in F.E. Hutchinson (ed.), *The Works of George Herbert*, p.xxi.
† Quoted in F.E. Hutchinson (ed.), *The Works of George Herbert*, p.xxxvii.

seventeenth-century literature has been more closely studied that it has been appreciated that Herbert took Donne's techniques and modified them with considerable ingenuity to make discoveries in form and metre that were uniquely his own, and that, as a consequence, he established a diction and style for religious poetry which directly influenced many other poets—for example, Vaughan, Traherne and Crashaw.

A comparison of Herbert with Donne points up strikingly how the Metaphysical style could accommodate a variety of major talents, and how Donne's example and influence did not have to be overwhelming. Herbert, of course, clearly owes much to Donne's innovative example: his verses demonstrate the introspection, the use of oblique conceits, unexpected metaphors, intellectual vigour and colloquial and dramatic language which we associate with Donne. Yet, on the other hand, the tension and display which are invariably to the forefront of Donne's verse are, in Herbert's poetry, generally contained or suppressed beneath a clear, lucid and transparent surface. A further point which illustrates the difference between these two fine poets is the distinctive stance each habitually adopts in any one poem: whereas Donne dramatises, uses poetry to work out an idea, and argues throughout the course of the work, Herbert appears more 'passive' and simply records a conflict that is now past, as for instance in 'The Pilgrimage'. In Herbert the drama or tension is all retrospective, since he writes from the vantage point of the resolution of a conflict, and his wit is redefined and controlled by the nature of his spiritual experience.

The distinction has consequences for Herbert's poetic idiom, its diction and figurative language. There are occasions, and the recollection of profound religious experience may be one, when simple speech is more forceful than anything which is more obviously intended to impress. Herbert clearly grasped this insight and his poetry is an eloquent demonstration of it. Although his religious subject is dressed in plain speech, it is given beauty in other ways, especially in sound. Herbert's poems are a striking demonstration of how he manipulated the rhythms and sounds of speech so that each poem could be a gracious musical instrument for his thought. As Dr Hutchinson has observed, 'Few English poets have been able to use the plain words of ordinary speech with a greater effect of simple dignity than Herbert.'* This is true of his general style which is not merely Metaphysical but also courtly and 'popular'. Behind this may stand something of the tradition of the Church and its sermons, which spills over into his homely analogies and illustrations, but it also suggests his grasp of an Elizabethan use of English where assonance and alliteration control emphasis to enforce a sense of natural speech. (An illustration of

* F.E. Hutchinson (ed.), *The Works of George Herbert*, p.L.

Herbert's use of assonance is the line 'Onely take this gentle rose' where the vowel sounds of the first word of the line are repeated in the last word.) This same line of development can be seen in the way Herbert uses figurative language. Compared with Donne his conceits appear simpler, and there is less obvious emphasis on 'strong lines'; but then his focus is directed away from himself and towards a divine reality, and, with this as his real subject, excessive display of learning and individual wit would be inappropriate. As a consequence it is natural that most of his conceits are drawn from nature or the Bible, and this feature gives his poems something of the aura of biblical parable and enhances the ring of authority, truth and certainty that is part of their total effect. This is most clearly demonstrated in such poems as 'Virtue' or 'The Flower'.

Herbert's ingenuity is displayed freely in his verse forms. He is a master of versification, one of the most accomplished in English poetry: his poems reveal an impressive variety of stanza forms where he continually experiments with patterns which will most appropriately reflect the content, whether merely the subject—as in 'Easter Wings' where the arrangement of the lines on the page presents a visual image of wings—or the more intricate movements of thought and recorded experience which are the essence of the poems 'Aaron', 'Sinnes Round' or 'The Collar'. The pattern poems, the name given to poems where lines represent some physical object, are often criticised as laboured artificial forms, but in 'The Altar' and 'Easter Wings' Herbert takes the form beyond a mere feat of ingenuity. In 'Easter Wings' the two movements of diminuendo and crescendo which allow the shape, also create an image for the fall and rise of the lark's song and for the fall and resurrection of man in Christ. In short, form and content here are inextricably interwoven.

For Herbert, the religious subject is the controlling element, and it is imperative that the reader should appreciate this. A fine critic of Herbert's work has commented that it is difficult to pretend any longer that 'the ideas and beliefs of a poet are of no importance in determining our response to his "aesthetic structure" ... It is now possible to treat seriously the thought of a seventeenth-century Christian without either apologies to the gods of inevitable progress, an air of bravura, or an attempt at literary psychoanalysis ... Today, as in the past, it is impossible to fully perceive or respond to Herbert's aesthetic achievement without an understanding of the religious thought and experience which is both its subject and its inspiration.'* The appearance of simplicity in Herbert's verse is deceptive and is achieved only by a great effort. It is founded upon a profound spiritual vision which

* Joseph H. Summers, *George Herbert: His Religion and Art*, Centre for Medieval and Early Renaissance Studies, New York, 1981 (first published 1954), p.27.

implies more than is ever said. Like Donne, Herbert demonstrates a 'unified sensibility' and reconciles opposite concepts, but by a certainty that the infinite can be comprehended in terms of simple, worldly things, rather than by a display of witty contortions. The point is well illustrated by Herbert's comments in the chapter of *A Priest to the Temple, or The Country Parson* where he gives advice about how the parson ought to teach his flock:

> This is the skill, and doubtlesse the Holy Scripture intends thus much, when it condescends to the naming of the plough, a hatchet, a bushell, leaven, boyes piping and dancing; shewing that things of ordinary use are not only to serve in the way of drudgery, but to be washed, and cleansed, and serve for lights even of Heavenly Truths.*

A further indication of Herbert's careful deflection of wit away from himself and towards God is found in the poem 'The Thanksgiving' where he proclaims that wit itself is to be seen as neither more nor less than the gift of God to the poet:

> If thou shalt give me wit, it shall appear,
> If thou hast giv'n it me, 'tis here.

The Temple: general features

Published by Nicholas Ferrar soon after Herbert's death in 1633, *The Temple* needs to be considered in terms of an all-encompassing architectural metaphor with biblical associations, in particular the verse 'Know ye not that ye are the temples of God, and that the Spirit of God dwelleth in you?' (1 Corinthians 3:16). It is in three parts: a long poem, 'The Church-porch', is followed by the numerous short lyrics of 'The Church', and, finally, the narrative 'The Church militant'.

The collection is organised in such a way as to be educational, and its logical development is reminiscent of a programme of pastoral spiritual instruction. This is especially true of 'The Church-porch'. This wide-ranging poem, which covers more than purely religious instruction, is concerned with the general moral teaching that should be understood and practised before one enters the church. The poem seems to be addressed to a general audience, and its tone is appropriately rational and commonsensical, rather than emotional, its content being the externals of Christian life and behaviour. In short, physically located outside the Church, on 'the porch', this poem prefaces the whole collection with the essentials upon which the remaining poems are based.

* Quoted in F.E. Hutchinson (ed.), *The Works of George Herbert*, p.257.

Since the organisation of the lyrics in the main part of the collection, 'The Church', is more complicated, appreciation of the order which has shaped the work requires more careful consideration. The focus of the poems is really upon the inner dimension of Christian experience, the relationship between Christ and the soul. The audience changes from poem to poem: it may be fellow Christians, Christ, or the speaker's soul. The dates for individual poems are generally undetermined, but the collection is so organised that it suggests a deepening spiritual awareness. Entrance to the collection is through the pattern poem 'The Altar'. By its reference to the altar, which is the focal point of the church, and its allusion to the sacrament of Holy Communion or Eucharist which is offered upon the altar (and which reminds the Christian of Christ's death on the cross, and unites the Christian with Christ), this poem establishes the spiritual context of the whole collection. Herbert arranges the lines of the poem to represent an altar: in this sense the poem is clearly a pattern poem. But the altar also becomes an emblem, in the manner of the emblem books which were so popular during the Renaissance (see below, p.86), as Herbert makes the hidden meaning of the visual image the basis of a meditation that is founded upon the conceit of the parallel between the stone altar and the human heart.

The other poems which follow are based upon other details of Church life and tradition. Some are organised by their meditation upon the seasons of the Church's calendar: this begins with Advent, which commemorates the coming of Christ, and continues with Christmas, Easter, Pentecost, the festival which commemorates the coming of the Holy Spirit upon the disciples soon after the Ascension of the Resurrected Christ, and the Sundays after Trinity Sunday which concentrate upon aspects of Church doctrine and life. Other poems reflect topics of specific religious instruction, church architecture and services, while a final grouping is concerned with the 'Last Things'—death, judgement and the life beyond.

At a time when the form of worship of the Established Church was under attack from the Puritans, Herbert's poems are a cogent and resolute celebration of the Christian calendar and the Church's worship. The versatility of his approach to the various means of devotion and meditation is impressive. He freely draws upon the vocal forms of hymns and prayer, especially the Psalms and the Bible. For example, 'The Sacrifice', with its use of dramatic monologue—something unusual in 'The Church'—is based upon the Good Friday liturgy. Yet Herbert also demonstrates his familiarity with the various forms and techniques of meditation, and, in some instances, his spiritual awareness hints at an experience of contemplative prayer, that is, prayer which attains a direct sense of the presence of God. Equally striking is Herbert's use of various visual forms (of which the pattern poems are but one obvious example) such as stained-glass windows, crucifixes and statues.

Although the final section, 'The Church militant', seems to have been begun at an earlier date than many of the other poems in the collection, it is structurally an integral part of *The Temple*. It complements the theme of 'The Church' with its focus upon the individual soul, by an historical exposition concentrating upon the development of the Church in history. This subject explains Herbert's title 'Church militant', since, in contrast to the Church Triumphant which refers to the believers who have died and are in heaven, the term applies to the Church on earth which is in warfare against 'the world, the flesh, and the devil'. This attempt at a perspective which might adequately present the divine plan for the universe is reminiscent of other ambitious attempts at a summary of Christian history, for instance Augustine's *City of God*, or Donne's *The Progress of the Soul*. As in the *City of God*, or indeed in the final books of *Paradise Lost* with Michael's vision of the future for Adam, Herbert advances a view of finite human history which is essentially pessimistic: after the Fall the world cannot be reclaimed by the Church, and it must instead, on the one hand, look towards individual salvation, and, on the other, towards the end of all things and God's Final Judgement.

'The Church-porch'

From the outset, the arrangement of Herbert's poems appears to be strongly influenced by his concern for religious instruction. The seventy-seven stanzas of 'The Church-porch' are primarily a substantial sequence of moral instructions in verse called the *Perirrhanterium*. This word is the Greek term for an instrument for sprinkling holy water, and it implies an act of purification, or the practical and moral preparations that are necessary before entering the church. The first stanza displays the element of moral instruction and desire to edify the reader which is such a characteristic of Herbert's approach here. He makes 'a bait of pleasure', so that while the reader will read for pleasure, he will also gain valuable instruction:

> Thou, whose sweet youth and early hopes inhance
> Thy rate and price, and mark thee for a treasure;
> Hearken unto a Verser, who may chance
> Ryme thee to good, and make a bait of pleasure.
>   A verse may finde him, who a sermon flies,
>   And turn delight into a sacrifice.

Direct and perceptive in a way that the lyrical poems seldom are, 'The

Church-porch' can be divided into sections, and its range of topics is considerable, including advice on chastity and temperance, education, the use of money and conversation. These details remind us that in ancient times the church porch was used as a place for the settling of accounts, and they clearly demonstrate how Herbert's spiritual vision is founded upon a fullness of response to life, in which body and soul are interrelated and the things of the spirit are ultimately bound to such details as those of manners and morals. For precedents in this type of writing Herbert could turn to Donne's 'Letters to severall Personages', or to the works of Elizabethan poets such as Southwell and Breton (?1545–?1626) who had used the same metre for similar moral 'pep-talks'.

'The Church'

Literary, biblical and liturgical influences

Who sayes that fictions onely and false hair
Become a verse? Is there in truth no beautie?
Is all good structure in a winding stair?
May no lines passe, except they do their dutie
    Not to a true, but painted chair?

Is it no verse, except enchanted groves
And sudden arbours shadow course-spunne lines?
Must purling streams refresh a lovers loves?
Must all be vail'd, while he that reades, divines,
    Catching the sense at two removes?

Shepherds are honest people; let them sing:
Riddle who list, for me, and pull for Prime:
I envie no mans nightingale or spring;
Nor let them punish me with loss of rime,
    Who plainly say, *My God, My King.* ('Jordan (I)')

The poems in 'The Church' demonstrate the various influences at work in Herbert's poetry and his consciousness of the literary context in which he wrote. The two 'Jordan' poems are outstanding examples of this particular aspect of the collection. Both poems can be read as Herbert's literary manifesto, a declaration of his independence from the artificial styles and conventions of the various literary traditions used by his predecessors, and of his commitment to religious poetry and to a bold and innovative 'realism' that would be appropriate to his subject. In the light of this, Herbert's title for these poems has considerable force, for the river Jordan is traditionally an image associated with baptism and ministry. In both the Old and New Testaments the river Jordan has immense religious significance: most important is the fact that it is where Christ was himself baptised—an act which marked the beginning of his mission and which established the association of Jordan and baptism. In symbolic terms, Jordan essentially marks a point of no return: it can denote the beginning of a new being (as in baptism), or death (entry into the 'Promised Land'), or some association derived from both these elements.

What is striking about 'Jordan (I)' is the way in which Herbert employs elaborate clichés to identify and criticise various contemporary literary styles. The first stanza alludes mainly, but not exclusively (see lines 9–10), to the complexity of Donne's Metaphysical style, while the second stanza turns to the artificiality of Elizabethan and Spenserian styles of pastoral and allegorical poetry. It is the third stanza in which Herbert declares his own style and subject for himself and displays that saintly realism which uses 'plain' speech as its means of expression.

The contrast with Donne extends further than the elimination of the 'winding stair' of obscure expression that Herbert refers to: it includes, and is most obvious in, the stance and tone that Herbert adopts. Where Donne twists and argues, is dramatic and immediate, Herbert's most characteristic style is one of direct statement. The dramatic element of his verse is a recreation of a past, but now resolved, conflict recalled in a tone of reflection. The effect is essentially non-dramatic, but at the same time, and precisely because the human perspective is subordinated, the effect is also to heighten the sense of a supernatural presence impressing upon the poet and charging every aspect of his life and all created things.

These points can be illustrated by reference to 'Jordan (II)', whose theme is the distinction between finite human understanding and an infinite divine reality. Herbert never disparages the human element. Indeed he celebrates it, and the creative and inventive processes which are part of nature as words and ideas, with such lush language as 'burnish, sprout, and swell'. But the point Herbert makes is that for a divine subject ('heav'nly joyes') even these refined tricks of wit are inappropriate: they obscure his meaning because they imply that God is accessible to human intellect—even if *only* in poetry:

When first my lines of heav'nly joyes made mention,
Such was their lustre, they did so excell,
That I sought out quaint words, and trim invention;
My thoughts began to burnish, sprout, and swell,
Curling with metaphors a plain intention,
Decking the sense, as if it were to sell.

Thousands of notions in my brain did runne,
Off'ring their service, if I were not sped:
I often blotted what I had begunne;
This was not quick enough, and that was dead.
Nothing could seem too rich to clothe the sunne,
Much lesse those joyes which trample on his head.

As flames do work and winde, when they ascend,
So did I weave my self into the sense.
But while I bustled, I might heare a friend
Whisper, *How wide is all this long pretence!*
There is in love a sweetnesse readie penn'd:
Copie out onely that, and save expense.

There is a gentle irony in the way in which the final stanza acts out the dilemma and contradiction: Herbert's verbal agility remains earth-bound—'I weave my self into the sense'—and he remains unable to express the essence of the divine presence. The resolution of the poem and a type of dramatic interest (though very different from Donne's) is achieved by Herbert's introduction of God as a voice speaking from beyond the body of the poem, a voice that cuts through the illusion with cool direct expression and a call to discipleship, *'Copie out onely that'*.

Forms of meditation and the religious life

Many of Donne's poems, like those of Herbert, bear clear indications of meditative and religious practices, but the style of Herbert's 'The Pilgrimage' is quite distinct and entirely free from the dramatic posturings and strong animal spirits which characterise Donne and endear him to many readers. In 'The Pilgrimage' Herbert adopts his distinctive, reflective stance of relative detachment, and fashions a poem which may almost be regarded as something of a manual of experience in the spiritual life. It accordingly wins a prominent place within the tradition of contemplative and mystical literature.

A recurrent theme of Herbert's poetry is demonstrated in this poem once more: that is, the fundamental contrast between what finite understanding may grasp and what spiritual illumination will reveal. The poem traces the poet's journey through life, as he purges himself of his misdirected intellectual and spiritual desires, and arrives at a point of illumination where he accepts renunciation and embraces the divine will. The imagery throughout is of the type associated with religious allegory—such as that of Spenser's *Faerie Queene* and the very popular *Pilgrim's Progress* by the Baptist tinker John Bunyan (1628–88). With its allusions to the 'cave of Desperation', the 'rock of

Pride', the 'wilde of Passion' and 'Fancies medow', the poem gives the various stages of the spiritual life an illusion of specific material reality—but it is an illusion which the reader is meant to see through and to *apply*:

I Travell'd on, seeing the hill where lay
    My expectation.
  A long it was and weary way.
  The gloomy cave of Desperation
I left on th' one, and on the other side
    The rock of Pride.

And so I came to Fancies medow strow'd
    With many a flower:
  Fain would I here have made abode,
  But I was quicken'd by my houre.
So to Cares cops I came, and there got through
    With much ado.

That led me to the wilde of Passion, which
    Some call the wold;
  A wasted place, but sometimes rich.
  Here I was robb'd of all my gold,
Save one good Angell, which a friend had ti'd
    Close to my side.

At length I got unto the gladsome hill,
    Where lay my hope,
  Where lay my heart; and climbing still,
  When I had gain'd the brow and top,
A lake of brackish waters on the ground
    Was all I found.

With that abash'd and struck with many a sting
    Of swarming fears,
  I fell, and cry'd, Alas my King!
  Can both the way and end be tears?
Yet taking heart I rose, and then perceiv'd
    I was deceiv'd:

My hill was further: so I flung away,
    Yet heard a crie
  Just as I went, *None goes that way*
  And lives: If that be all, said I,
After so foul a journey death is fair,
    And but a chair.

Here rhetoric and dramatic force have been deployed to aid in the exposition of a spiritual theme. Much of the power of this relatively abstract instruction lies in Herbert's manipulation of stanza forms in order to generate emotional vigour and interest. The radically shortened second and sixth lines illustrate this, as do the shorter third and fourth lines which are adjusted in order to carry different emotional stresses. So, for example, in the fourth stanza the emotional weight of 'where lay my hope' is carried on and over into the third line through the alliterative force of 'where lay my heart', and the sense of desolation and grief is correspondingly enhanced. In the last stanza, the resolution is achieved, as it is in 'Jordan (II)', by having the divine presence speak from beyond the poem, and the end of the quest is clearly affirmed as only being attainable beyond the grave.

Hieroglyphic poetry—church architecture

The most obvious example of the influence of visual concepts upon Herbert is his use of the pattern poem. The much cited 'Easter Wings' and 'The Altar' are, however, merely ostentatious examples of what was a more general interest on Herbert's part in types of hieroglyphic allusion. (A hieroglyph may be defined as 'a figure, device or sign having some hidden meaning; a secret or enigmatic symbol; an emblem.')* Herbert is not intrinsically innovative in his approach: the seventeenth century was accustomed to visual references of this sort, as can be seen in the various popular emblem books and the poems written for them, such as those by Francis Quarles (1592–1644). A poem such as 'The Altar' demonstrates Herbert's ability to manipulate an established and still popular genre—the emblem—and it is worth noticing that George Puttenham (?1530–90) in his *The Arte of English Poesie* (1589) devotes a chapter to the pattern poem and its 'ocular representation'.

The use of emblems marks the habit of thought in a period which cast about for correspondences between things, greater and lesser, and which saw nature—the world—as a series of interlocking systems, all of which constituted, as it were, one huge emblem which could direct the human soul toward the knowledge of God. While the device could serve to exhibit a poet's wit, its use was always to establish striking connections between disparate things through the emblem's visual (and verbal) metaphor. This, in turn, would be systematically elucidated, point by point. The meaning could be highly personal and enigmatic, or, as in the case of religious poets, it would be generally established by Christian tradition and scripture.

In various poems Herbert uses strategies which directly recall or employ the emblem. However, his adaptations show that he never uses

* *Compact Oxford English Dictionary*, Oxford University Press, New York, 1971, p.1303.

the method in a crude fashion but wittily twists it so that the reader is also surprised by the application. This can be seen in 'The Church-floore' where the reader is led to expect a moral interpretation which applies the theological virtues to architectural details, but is surprised by the final couplet which shows that Herbert has really being talking about the human heart. It is typical of Herbert that the surprise lies in his personal method, and that the institution of the Church has been shown to be an emblem of the individual soul rather than vice versa:

> Blest be the *Architect*, whose art
> Could build so strong in a weak heart.

Within his work other examples of this strategic use of emblems include 'The Bunch of Grapes', 'Joseph's coat', 'Sinnes round', 'A Wreath', 'Trinitie Sunday', 'Deniall' and 'Aaron'—this list is not exhaustive. All are dependent upon symbolic meanings well establish-ed within the Christian tradition. The commonest application of the emblem is either as the image which the poem explains, or the image which explains the poem. Invariably the formal structure of the poem is part of the meaning and is intimately related to the organisation of the subject, so that logic, rhythm and rhyme are related and lead to the final resolution. For example, in 'Deniall', the opening broken stanzas reflect spiritual disorder, and the final movement into rhyme marks the resolution of the poem in which rebellion has been replaced by acquies-ence and the restoration of order.

In some instances the courtly interest in diverse forms of wit, such as acrostics (where letters of each line form a word or saying) and ana-grams (where letters can be rearranged to form another word or phrase) form part of the emblem; and even typography may also matter, as in 'Paradise'. These occasions, which often involve a wrenching of customary spelling, veer towards the extremes of the pattern poem *per se* and its inherent dangers of artificiality. While these forms are now so remote from a modern reader's experience that they can be difficult to appreciate, a reader should remember that Her-bert consistently saw the poem as an integrated representation of a spiritual mystery: these devices were designed wittily to combine the spiritual and the material, the rational and the aesthetic, in such a way that they would not only be united, but the reader would be provoked to contemplate the subject deeply. The fundamental purpose was didactic: such poems aimed to stimulate the reader's powers of reason, or wit, and thereby induce the reader to decipher the clues of existence and so ultimately lead him back to the adoration of God. The context of this approach was a well-established one, as can be seen by the remarks of Sir Philip Sidney:

Neither let it be deemed too saucy a comparison, to balance the highest point of man's wit with the efficacy of nature; but rather give right honour to the heavenly Maker of that maker, who having made man to his own likeness, set him beyond and over all the works of that second nature; which in nothing he showeth so much as in poetry; when, with the force of a divine breath, he bringest things forth surpassing her doings, with no small arguments to the incredulous of that first accursed fall of Adam; since our erected wit maketh us know what perfection is, and yet our infected will keepeth us from reaching unto it.*

'Church-monuments' has been greatly admired by most critics. The poem is a superb display both of how Herbert utilises the emblem but is not contained by it, and how firmly he concentrates its resources to assist his religious vision. Critics have remarked on Herbert's artful use of rhyme, enjambment (the continuation of a sentence beyond the end of a line) and flexible syntax. Perhaps the most fulsome praise has been that of Yvor Winters who has acclaimed it as Herbert's 'greatest poem'. Winters remarks: 'George Herbert's *Church Monuments*, perhaps the most polished and urbane poem of the Metaphysical School and one of the half dozen most profound, is written in an iambic pentameter line so carefully modulated, and with its rhymes so carefully concealed at different and unexpected points in the syntax, that the poem suggests something of the quiet plainness of excellent prose without losing the organisation and variety of verse.'†

However, Winters fails to see the poem's dependence upon the tradition of emblem poetry, although the subject demands it be read as such. The poem is a type of meditation upon death, a *memento mori*. The immediate focus of the meditation is upon the monuments which decorate the tombs within the church and the hieroglyphic meanings which can be drawn from them:

While that my soul repairs to her devotion,
Here I intombe my flesh, that it betimes
May take acquaintance of this heap of dust;
To which the blast of deaths incessant motion,
Fed with the exhalation of our crimes,
Drives all at last. Therefore I gladly trust

My bodie to this school, that it may learn
To spell his elements, and finde his birth

* *The Defence of Poetry.* Quoted in William Gray (ed.), *The Miscellaneous Works*, Boston, 1860, pp.69-70.
† Quoted by Joseph Summers, *George Herbert: His Religion and Art*, p.132.

Written in dustie heraldrie and lines;
Which dissolution sure doth best discern,
Comparing dust with dust, and earth with earth.
These laugh at Jeat and Marble put for signes,

To sever the good fellowship of dust,
And spoil the meeting. What shall point out them,
When they shall bow, and kneel, and fall down flat
To kiss those heaps, which now they have in trust?
Deare flesh, while I do pray, learn here thy stemme
And true descent; that when thou shalt grow fat,

And wanton in thy cravings, thou mayest know,
That flesh is but the glasse, which holds the dust
That measures all our time; which also shall
Be crumbled into dust. Mark here below
How tame these ashes are, how free from lust,
That thou mayest fit thy self against thy fall.

The first stanza declares the meditative purpose of the poem, but the focus of the meditation swiftly moves beyond the particular flesh to encompass the whole process of decay and reveal the futility of such finite attempts to arrest the process of dissolution as the monuments represent. Herbert's careful craftsmanship makes the poem itself an emblem. This is clearly demonstrated by his use of enjambment and syntax to break down the individuality and sense of separateness of each stanza, and in doing so he mirrors the process of dissolution which both the flesh and its memorials must endure. Joseph Summers has described this process elegantly: 'The sentences sift down through the rhyme-scheme skeleton of the stanzas like the sand through the glass; and the glass itself has already begun to crumble.'* The process and its controlling idea are condensed in this image of the hour-glass. All created things, flesh and monuments, are 'but the glasse, which holds the dust/ That measures all our time'. Again the edifying purpose of the meditation is clear. Once more the world is perceived as an emblem or hieroglyph which the discerning reader 'may learn to spell' —that is, in the immediate tangible sense of tracing out and deciphering the obscure inscriptions on the monuments themselves, and also ultimately in the sense of comprehending spiritual reality. This theme is a recurring favourite with Herbert; it appears, for instance, with similar meaning in 'The Flower' where he remarks 'Thy word is all, if we could spell.'

* Joseph Summers, *George Herbert: His Religion and Art*, p.134.

The Church's calendar

It has been estimated that about a quarter of the poems in *The Temple* are directly concerned with music, and in his account of Herbert's life Izaak Walton emphasises what a crucial place music held in Herbert's life. He records how Herbert left Bemerton twice a week to visit Salisbury Cathedral to play music with a group of his friends there, and gives a vivid account of Herbert's last Sunday alive, describing how he rose from his bed to tune an instrument and sing one of his own compositions. Walton's *Life* also affirms the value the Church's calendar held for Herbert with its annual and daily cycles for hymns and psalms. A number of his poems directly reflect this, and the daily cycle is represented by the poems 'Mattens' and 'Even-song'. Herbert's advice to the country parson included that he should encourage parishoners to sing 'Psalms at their work and on Holy days', and in his own calling as a parish priest he would have been intimate with the services of the Church and their choral settings—these are influences which lie behind 'Mattens', 'Even-song', 'The H. Communion', 'Christmas', 'Easter' and 'Whitsunday'. Indeed critics and musicologists have pointed out how Herbert's intimate knowledge of music provided more than a field of imagery and allusion for his poetry; they have shown that the musical values of dissonance, cadence, pitch and the essentials of polyphony are deeply embedded into the structure of many of his poems. As a source of imagery, Herbert's use of music, and his ability to fuse it with such commonplaces as the idea of a universal harmony, is well demonstrated in these stanzas from 'Providence':

> Beasts fain would sing; birds dittie to their notes;
> Trees would be tuning on their native lute
> To thy renown: but all their hands and throats
> Are brought to Man, while they are lame and mute.

> Man is the worlds high Priest: he doth present
> The sacrifice for all; while they below
> Unto the service mutter an assent,
> Such as springs use that fall, and windes that blow.

The poem 'Christmas' is a good example of Herbert's consciousness both of the Church's music and what made that music possible: the order of the Christian calendar with its major festivals. Herbert's own theology is generally dependent upon a high theology of the Eucharist, the service of Holy Communion, and the ideas of the transformation of simple elements, such as bread and wine, into means of spiritual grace. The implications of this are far reaching: where he is not specifically Eucharistic he is almost invariably concerned with what theologians term charitology, which is concerned with the operation of the grace of God and the transformation of the soul under that grace. For Herbert the Eucharist is the chief example of how divine grace can transform physical things, such as bread and wine, to make them spiritually significant, and that this prefigures the transformation of the human soul under the grace of God, received through sharing in the Sacrament of the Eucharist. Again Herbert's celebration of these festivals shows him to be within the position generally followed by the Established Church, and opposed to the reformist views of Puritan and Presbyterian sections. The debate was intense during his lifetime, as can be gauged from a letter by Joseph Hall upon the subject where he remarks:

> For the celebration of the solemn Feasts of our Saviour's Nativity, Resurrection, Ascension, and the Coming Down of the Holy Ghost, which you say is cried down by your zealous Lecturer, one would think there should be reason enough in those wonderful and unspeakable benefits which those days serve to commemorate unto us ... *

The structure of 'Christmas' is twofold. The first part is a type of dramatic speech, a sonnet, and the second is a song, with the interest lying in the contrast between the two parts and their different forms. Herbert's method here can be compared to other similar poems, in particular 'Easter' and 'An Offering'. In the sonnet he provides an allegorical account of spiritual experience—much as in the manner of 'Pilgrimage'. He describes how in the course of life he is drawn to Christ through his awareness of the insufficiency of any created thing —'the grief/ Of pleasures brought me to him.' The first part then expands with a general ejaculation or prayer to the incarnate Christ where the infinite is telescoped into the manger—'Oh Thou whose glorious yet contracted light ... '. The meditation is then personally applied: 'Furnish & deck my soul'. In that closing section the poem, with its exposition, meditation and petition, stands complete as a meditative sonnet. But with the second part, we find that the sonnet has merely been an act of preparation for a hymn, and the mood changes from meditation and petition to sung vocal praise:

> All after pleasures as I rid one day,
>   My horse and I, both tir'd, bodie and minde,
>   With full crie of affections, quite astray,
> I took up in the next inne I could finde.
> There when I came, whom found I but my deare,
>   My dearest Lord, expecting till the grief
>   Of pleasures brought me to him, readie there

---

* Quoted in P.E. More and F.L. Cross (eds), *Anglicanism*, S.P.C.K., London, 1935, p.577.

To be all passengers most sweet relief?
O Thou, whose glorious, yet contracted light,
   Wrapt in nights mantle, stole into a manger;
   Since my dark soul and brutish is thy right,
To Man of all beasts be not thou a stranger:
   Furnish & deck my soul, that thou mayst have
   A better lodging then a rack or grave.

The shepherds sing; and shall I silent be?
   My God, no hymne for thee?
My soul's a shepherd too; a flock it feeds
   Of thoughts, and words, and deeds.
The pasture is thy word: the streams, thy grace
   Enriching all the place.
Shepherd and flock shall sing, and all my powers
   Out-sing the day-light houres.
Then we will chide the sunne for letting night
   Take up his place and right:
We sing one common Lord; wherefore he should
   Himself the candle hold.
I will go searching, till I finde a sunne
   Shall stay, till we have done;
A willing shiner, that shall shine as gladly,
   As frost-nipt sunnes look sadly.
Then we will sing, and shine all our own day,
   And one another pay:
His beams shall cheer my breast, and both so twine,
Till ev'n his beams sing, and my musick shine.

The song section (lines 15–34) is well known for its having been set to music by Vaughan Williams (1872–1958) in *Hodie: A Christmas Cantata* (1953). Essentially the song duplicates the movement of the first section but also moves beyond it. Where the meditation concluded with a petition for the union of the soul with God, the hymn concludes with an assumption that such a union will take place. In short, the music raises poet and song to another level of spiritual awareness.

   The song begins with a call to praise on the occasion of the festival, and uses bright but traditional—even archetypal—images which recall the role of the parish priest and his parishioners. Over all is the brilliant light of the sun, again an archetypal light rather than the watery beams of a northern hemisphere sun in winter. Herbert surprises the reader's expectations by deflecting the image of sheep and shepherd from pastor and parish to his own soul where the flock are his 'thoughts, and words, and deeds'. The effect is to suggest a unity of being, a summing up of all Herbert's powers in a single act of praise. The shift of thought is that praise of God requires an eternity of light and that the search for such a 'willing shiner' implies both the perpetual light of eternity and the felicity of grace that will exist between this light of God and the poet's soul where 'both so twine./ Till ev'n his beams sing, and my musick shine.'

The Last Things

Traditional subjects for religious poetry were the imminence of death and the prospect of judgement, heaven and hell. Donne's *Holy Sonnets* are well known examples of meditations upon such things, and Herbert, too, provides examples of the subject. 'The Forerunners' can be seen within this tradition, but it is more than merely a set-piece meditation. In fact, it needs to be compared with the two 'Jordan' poems more than anything else. Here, as in the 'Jordan' poems, Herbert is considering his poetic achievement:

> The harbingers are come. See, see their mark;
> White is their colour, and behold my head.
> But must they have my brain? must they dispark
> Those sparkling notions, which therein were bred?
>   Must dulnesse turn me to a clod?
> Yet have they left me, *Thou art still my God.*
>
> Good men ye be, to leave me my best room,
> Ev'n all my heart, and what is lodged there:
> I passe not, I, what of the rest become,
> So *Thou art still my God*, be out of fear.
>   He will be pleased with that dittie;
> And if I please him, I write fine and wittie.
>
> Farewell sweet phrases, lovely metaphors.
> But will ye leave me thus? when ye before
> Of stews and brothels onely knew the doores,
> Then did I wash you with my tears, and more,
>   Brought you to Church well drest and clad:
> My God must have my best, ev'n all I had.
>
> Lovely enchanting language, sugar-cane,
> Hony of roses, whither wilt thou flie?
> Hath some fond lover tic'd thee to thy bane?
> And wilt thou leave the Church, and love a stie?
>   Fie, thou wilt soil thy broider'd coat,
> And hurt thy self, and him that sings the note.
>
> Let foolish lovers, if they will love dung,
> With canvas, not with arras, clothe their shame:

Let follie speak in her own native tongue.
True beautie dwells on high: ours is a flame
    But borrow'd thence to light us thither.
Beautie and beauteous words should go together.

Yet if you go, I passe not; take your way:
For, *Thou art still my God*, is all that ye
Perhaps with more embellishment can say.
Go birds of spring: let winter have his fee;
    Let a bleak palenesse chalk the doore,
So all within be livelier then before.

The difference between this poem and the 'Jordan' poems lies in its place in Herbert's life, for here Herbert is considering his work in the light of advancing age and approaching death. The 'Jordan' poems were marked by a forced and conscious rejection of other styles in favour of simplicity, and the simple 'My God, My King' was exclaimed *instead of* wit or lyric sweetness. But now, in 'The Forerunners', the clash between form and content is transcended. Depth of meaning has been hammered into simplicity—so that the poem is both about growing old and writing poetry—and allows us to gauge the measure of Herbert's growth as a poet.

The poem is enfolded by the conceit of a royal progress for which advance messengers secured accommodation by chalking the doors. Here, of course, the progress is God's, and the messengers have marked the progress by whitening Herbert's hair. The fear is that he will have no wits left to welcome his God, but he finds that he is left indeed with the one vital phrase, which recurs throughout the poem, and with his best room—his heart.

The struggle for wit in piety, for divine beauty to receive beauteous words, remains with him – a shadow of the earlier conflict between the university orator and the priest. Here the resolution is achieved with the realisation that the beauty of the soul and the beauty of expression exist only upon condition of the recognition that they are 'But borrow'd'. In short, the poet must be prepared to surrender them when called. The simplicity that Herbert attains is the reverse of naivety, but rather the consequence of an enormous concentration of complex awareness, life and energy, to produce an art which lays upon the reader the imperative which Rilke affirmed: 'You must change your life.'*

* 'Du musst dein Leben ändern'; 'Archaîscher Torso Apollos,' in M.D. Herter Norton's *Translations from the Poetry of Rainer Maria Rilke*, New York, 1938, pp.180–1.

Chapter 6
Richard Crashaw

Life

> What he might eate or weare he tooke no thought.
> His needfull foode he rather found then sought.
> He seekes no downes, no sheetes, his bed's still made.
> If he can find a chaire or stoole, he's layd,
> When day peepes in, he quitts his restlesse rest.
> And still, poore soule, before he's vp he's dres't.
> Thus dying did he liue, yet liued to dye
> In th' virgines lappe, to whom he did applye
> His virgine thoughts and words, and thence was styld
> By foes, the chaplaine of the virgine myld
> While yet he liued without: His modestie
> Imparted this to some, and they to me.*

These posthumous remarks by Richard Crashaw's close personal friend, Thomas Car (1599–1674), also an English convert to Roman Catholicism, and a priest, should not be taken lightly as a merely complimentary instance of obituary. Car's testimony to Crashaw (?1612–49) is consistent with a substantial body of literary evidence which shows Crashaw to have been highly regarded as a man of sincere belief —even saintliness—and considerable personal charm. Cowley, for instance, wrote an accomplished poem in honour of Crashaw, first published in 1656, which contains a daring conceit that compares Crashaw's admirable qualities as a man with the miracle of the Incarnation in which God took human form in Christ:

> *Poet* and *Saint*! to thee alone are given
> The two most sacred *Names* of *Earth* and *Heav'en*
> The hard and rarest *Union* which can be
> Next that of *Godhead* with *Humanitie*...†

---

*'Crashawe the Anagramme He Was Car'. Quoted in L.C. Martin (ed.), *The Poems of Richard Crashaw*, Clarendon Press, Oxford, 1977, p.234. Unless otherwise indicated all quotations from Crashaw, including the peculiarities of spelling and typography, are taken from this edition.

† Quoted in L.C. Martin (ed.), *The Poems of Richard Crashaw*, p.XL.

Another revealing illustration of the high regard in which Crashaw was held are the sentiments of the unidentified author of 'The Preface to the Reader' (probably Joseph Beaumont (1616–99) since the florid style is reminiscent of his own and, like Crashaw, he had been a Fellow of Peterhouse from 1636 to 1644) in *Steps to the Temple* (1646) where he refers to Crashaw's scholarly accomplishments, in languages, music, poetry and drawing, and his devotion *'in St.* Maries *Church neere St.* Peters *Colledge'* and his *'rare moderation in diet'*.*

What background or genetic factors go to make a personality as sensitive and complex as Crashaw must remain conjecture. Such information as we possess is suggestive, even remarkable, if not conclusive. For instance, in view of Crashaw's later development, it is fascinating to find that his father, William Crashaw (1572–1626), was a prominent Puritan divine, the author of various devotional and controversial works, and, even more remarkable, was especially noted for his hatred of Popery and the Jesuits—as is clear from his remarks in his will:

> I accounte Poperie . . . the heape and chaos of all heresies and the channell whereinto the fowlest impieties & heresies y^t have byne in the christian Worlde have runn and closelye emptied themselues. I beleeue the Popes seate and power to be the power of the greate Antechrist and the doctrine of the Pope . . . to be the doctrine of Antechriste. yea that doctrine of Divells prophecied of by the Apostle and that the true and absolute Papist soe livinge and dyeinge debarrs himself of salvation for oughte that we knowe . . .†

It is certain that Crashaw's father had a substantial theological library, and we can assume that, perhaps even more than in the case of Donne or Herbert, Crashaw was widely read in the literature of devotion and theology from an early age. It would be naive, however, to leap to the conclusion, however tantalising, that Crashaw's subsequent conversion to Roman Catholicism was a direct reaction against his father: it has been pointed out that 'all the son's characteristics of imagination, style and piety are foreshadowed in the father.'‡

In terms of his education, Crashaw seems to have been fortunate. Though it is not known where he first went to school, he entered the Charterhouse in 1629 (at this time, his father having died, he was under the guardianship of two lawyers, one of whom was a governor of the school). Here he was fortunate in having as his headmaster Robert Brook, who prescribed exercises in imitation of the classical orators and poets. Crashaw commemorated him in a tribute which prefixed the

---

* Quoted in L.C. Martin (ed.), *The Poems of Richard Crashaw*, p.76.
† Quoted in L.C. Martin (ed.), *The Poems of Richard Crashaw*, pp.xviii–xix.
‡ L. Bouyer, *A History of Christian Spirituality*, Burns & Oates, London, 1969, Vol. 3, p.134.

collection of Latin epigrams, *Epigrammatum Sacrorum* (1634).* Any firm dating of Crashaw's poems, particularly those written during his youth, presents problems. It is reasonable, however, to suppose that some of the epigrams written during the course of his academic exercises eventually found their way into this collection.

In 1634 Crashaw entered Pembroke College, Cambridge, where he commenced his Bachelor of Arts studies. At this time Pembroke was a centre of Laudian Anglicanism, as was Peterhouse of which Crashaw was elected a Fellow in 1636. There seems little doubt that the High Church doctrines favoured by Laud and his followers in the Established Church were among the decisive influences upon Crashaw during his time in Cambridge, and that these influences were varied enough for him to have access to various traditions and schools in theology and the spiritual life. During Crashaw's time Peterhouse was at the very centre of the Laudian revival, and its Master, Cosin (1595–1672), had introduced so many liturgical and devotional alterations, such as a crucifix and stained glass windows, that the notorious pamphleteering Puritan, William Prynne (1600–69), complained of its 'Popish ceremonies' and claimed that 'the common report was that none might approach the altar in Peterhouse but in sandals'† (sandals, of course, being the footwear of monks and friars). Cosin was the compiler of a book of liturgical offices, *A Collection of Private Devotions* (1627), and this work points up well the High Church theology and devotion which Crashaw would have encountered at Peterhouse. But there was more: nearby was the community of Little Gidding and Nicholas Ferrar, who was an assiduous collector of devotional books. Through Ferrar and the community Crashaw would have encountered the ritual of liturgy and a tradition of Catholic devotion which he later described in a poem which recalls Little Gidding's Anglican religious community, 'Description of a Religious House and Condition of Life'. In short, Crashaw was not restricted to any one spiritual tradition, and had no need to be. Also he was busy, as an Anglican priest and Curate of Little St Mary's from 1639, and as a Fellow of Peterhouse, and had the opportunity to test the various influences available to him against what his reason and practical experience could prove.

Sympathetic though he was to the High Church rituals of the Laudian reformers, and despite being more extreme and aesthetically influenced in these matters than Herbert‡, Crashaw might never have

---

* See L.C. Martin (ed.), *The Poems of Richard Crashaw*, p.10

† William Prynne, *Canterburies Doome*, London, 1646, p.73. Quoted in Austin Warren, *Richard Crashaw: A Study in Baroque Sensibility*, University of Michigan Press, Ann Arbor, 1957, p.33–4.

‡ See, for example, Herbert's description of 'The Parson's Church', Chapter XIII of *A Priest to the Temple or, The Country Parson*. Quoted in F.E. Hutchinson (ed.), *The Works of George Herbert*, pp.246–7.

converted to Roman Catholicism had he not felt compelled by the events of the Civil War. From the outset Crashaw's sympathies seem to have been with the King, and he appears as one of the Fellows of Peterhouse who combined to guarantee a loan of sixty pounds to the King in July 1642. But in 1643 the Puritan forces occupied Cambridge. Crashaw, who had realised that his position was dangerous, fled to Europe. This appears to have been a ruse to avoid his having to accept the Covenant (the 'solemn league and covenant' enforced by the Scottish Presbyterians in 1643 to resist the encroachments of Charles I on their religious liberty) and to ensure by his absence that he still retained his Fellowship. The effort was, of course, futile; and in his absence Crashaw was ejected from his Fellowship in April 1644, and was subsequently forced to begin the period of poverty and insecurity which characterised the last six years of his life.

These final years were based in Europe. In February 1643/4 Crashaw was in Holland, as is indicated by a surviving letter to members of the Little Gidding community. The letter's contents encouraged Crashaw's editor to remark that 'It is not hard to believe that his troubles were already encouraging him to take the step, which he must have taken by 1646, of seeking admission into the Roman Communion.'* The evidence suggests that sometime during 1645 Crashaw took up residence in Paris, where Queen Henrietta Maria and the English Court were in exile, and at about the same time, through the good offices of the Countess of Denbigh, he secured a recommendation to the Pope. This was in the form of a letter dated 7 September 1646, and it shows that his conversion must have taken place in 1645 at the latest. However, it took a long time for such influence as the Queen still had in Rome to achieve any result for Crashaw, who was then reduced to great poverty and ill-health; and it was only in 1647 that a post was made for him under Cardinal Palotto. Finally, in April 1649, he was given a minor post at the Cathedral of the Santa Casa at Loreto and died on 21 August the same year.

Crashaw and the Metaphysicals

Readers and critics of Crashaw have commonly shared a problem of where to place him amongst the literary fashions of the period. Though he is invariably associated with Herbert and the Metaphysicals, it is difficult to avoid the suspicion that this placement is convenient rather than necessarily convincing. The problem is that Crashaw's style is so markedly more emotional and unrestrained; the principles by which he gives order to his work can be difficult to identify, and are certainly

* L.C. Martin (ed.), *The Poems of Richard Crashaw*, p.xxvii.

less recognisable than they are in the poetry of either Donne or Herbert.

There are resemblances, of course, between Crashaw's works and the main Metaphysical line of Donne and Herbert. An obvious illustration of this is the way Crashaw clearly acknowledged his indebtedness to Herbert, and commemorated that affiliation by the choice of title for his first volume of sacred poems, *Steps to the Temple* (1646). In the preface of that work Crashaw is described by Beaumont as 'Herbert's *second, but equall, who hath retriv'd Poetry of late, and return'd it up to its Primitive use'*. * In precisely what aspect Crashaw is indebted to Herbert is controversial: perhaps in his use of simple language and homely images for devotional poetry. Most likely Beaumont's remark was intended to acknowledge Herbert's mastery in sacred lyric poetry—rather than to state anything more definite. Certainly, the extent of Herbert's influence must not be exaggerated, for it is obvious that Crashaw's dependence upon Herbert is far less than that of, say, Vaughan. The unmistakable influences are few: Crashaw's 'Charitas Nimia' suggests something of Herbert's manner and tone, while his 'On Mr G. Herberts booke intituled the Temple of Sacred Poems, sent to a Gentlewoman' is a graceful tribute in tetrameter couplets in the style of Jonson. This poem echoes Herbert's intimate style of speech, which Crashaw also transforms by his use of the tone and Petrarchan flattery of the Cavalier poets, and the way he playfully implies an amorous interest in the lady of the poem. His use of Donne is even less clear, but Donne's highly unified and intellectual treatment of the conceit is recalled in 'Loves Horoscope'.

Crashaw's distinctiveness may be illustrated by examining one crucial aspect of the Metaphysical style, the conceit, and comparing his conceits with those of Donne and Herbert. In the most simple terms the difference is that between the Metaphysical and Baroque styles, the Baroque being that transition in Europe, especially Italy, after about 1600, from the Renaissance style to a more elaborate, exuberant, comprehensive and consciously artificial form of art which penetrated into architecture, music, painting and letters. The Metaphysical conceit looks back to the Renaissance world: it is based upon the ancient philosophical notion of correspondences, and, at its best, gives a sense of philosophical exploration. Despite their immense differences, both Donne and Herbert treat the conceit in this way and use it as the organising principle or idea for a poem. As such, it is directly related to the actual subject of the poem upon which it focuses and which it clarifies and illustrates. When used in this way the conceit establishes the boundaries of the poem and acts as a discipline upon the emotions: for

---

* Quoted in L.C. Martin (ed.), *The Poems of Richard Crashaw*, p.75.

example, it ensures that Donne's emotions are never separated from his intellectual concerns and it fixes Herbert's devotion within the context of simple objects and the things of the earth.

This is not the case with Crashaw, whose conceits are more typically 'Baroque'. The 'Baroque' conceit does not explore or analyse, but views a symbol or paradox from various aspects, recapitulating, expanding and revising in a series of elaborations until some emotional truth emerges. Consequently, Crashaw's use of the conceit is, superficially, ornamental rather than functional. His conceit, of course, has a purpose, but it is an emotional rather than an intellectual one; it enriches and embellishes, rather than clarifies. The effect is perceived when the whole poem is seen as an image, or an architectural structure in the Baroque style—the image recalls Crashaw's own words: 'Love's architecture is his own.'*

As a devotional poet who is also a 'Metaphysical', Crashaw offers a further contrast with Donne, Herbert and Vaughan. Where these others are engaged in recording, analysing and comprehending the private fluctuations of the spiritual life, Crashaw's sensuous and exuberant celebrations are far more 'public' in focus. Instead of following their forms of private analysis, he contemplates the traditional paradoxes of faith and the spiritual life with awe and wonder, and celebrates the rituals and devotions of the Church. Crashaw shows little interest in the themes of hell, predestination or death, which haunt the other English devotional poets who have to write more directly against the context of the Puritan reformers, but instead he is much more concerned with stimulating an uplifted spiritual vision. In this emphasis there is an unexpected objectivity, since by it Crashaw also reflects the outward, social and cultural nature of the Baroque style.

The Baroque

It has been claimed for Crashaw that he 'represents a special phase in the history of European poetry, but he also transcends it'.†The view is well established. In fact, Crashaw reflects the uniqueness of the period from the 1590s through to, at least, the Commonwealth. As far as English literature is concerned, it was these years when what had taken two hundred years on the Continent was compressed into about fifty or sixty in England. During this time, condensed and repeated, all the various styles and phases of the European Renaissance—Renaissance, Mannerist and Baroque—intermingled inseparably.

---

* 'In The Holy Nativity of Our Lord God: A Hymn sung as by the Shepheards'.
† L.C. Martin (ed.), *The Poems of Richard Crashaw*, p.xxxviii.

English poet though he is, Crashaw's sensibility, his literary style and his spirituality, appear more Continental than English. Indeed, of all the English poets Crashaw appears the only one for whom the slippery term 'Baroque' is apposite: in the words of Douglas Bush, 'Crashaw is the one conspicuous English incarnation of the "Baroque sensibility".'*

The origins of the Baroque style lie in the spirituality of the Counter-Reformation when the Roman Catholic Church sought to reassert its authority after the Protestant Reformation, particularly through the doctrinal promulgations of the Council of Trent (1551). As such, the style is a cultural and spiritual assertion of confidence: theatrical, spectacular and propagandistic in nature, it is incomplete without an audience. Its essential impulse was to attempt to realise the spiritual in and through the sensuous by the multiplication and exhaustion of sensory impressions, and, in its various modes—sensuous, exuberant, grandiose, agitated—lines and forms are transcended by the pressure to move beyond the limits of any one medium or genre. This is demonstrated by the popularity of the emblem books in Catholic and also Protestant circles during the sixteenth and seventeenth centuries. Although these books precede the Baroque, their combination of text and illustration harmonised with the essentials of the Baroque style. Usually the emblems employed were traditional allegories, personifications or abstractions for various spiritual conditions with a motto or poem explaining the picture. It is interesting to see how many of these traditional forms accommodated themselves to the Baroque spirit. This can be illustrated by the way some emblems tended to translate the spiritual into literal, sensual and even palpable terms, as for instance when Christ is shown to be knocking at the door of a heart. This same literalness, which reaches toward the spiritual through the sensual and palpable, is an outstanding feature of Crashaw's last collection of religious poems, *Carmen Deo Nostro*, in which he includes various engravings, two of which he is believed to have sketched himself.

The dynamism of the Baroque style is most obvious in the visual arts, for example in the powerful sculptures of Giovanni Lorenzo Bernini (1598–1680) and the audacious ecclesiastical architecture of Borromini (1599–1667) and Rainaldi (1611–91). A most striking example of this is Bernini's enormous *Baldacchino* which canopies the altar beneath the dome of St Peter's in Rome. This canopy is huge, elaborately decorated and supported by huge columns covered in gold. The ornamentation is complex and tends to confuse the observer if he or she isolates and concentrates upon any one detail. But, if taken

* Douglas Bush, *English Literature in the Earlier Seventeenth Century*, Clarendon Press, Oxford, second edition, 1962, p.147.

within the whole context of the basilica, the *Baldacchino* is an awesome and bold spiritual statement which symbolises the spiralling of human aspiration upward towards the domed and vaulted harmonies of a perfect mathematical form—the dome itself. The inherent dangers of the style are obvious: the restless and unstable aspirations of the ornamental impulse culminated in the effusive Rococo style which succeeded the Baroque, a style which demonstrates the consequences when Baroque forms of expression lacked a sustaining aesthetic or spiritual principle to control them.

Baroque spirituality

The essence of the Baroque spirit is the attempt to realise the spiritual through the sensuous, and it is epitomised by, though not limited to, the theology and spirituality of the Counter-Reformation with its emphasis upon the senses in ritual, the doctrine of transubstantiation in which the bread and wine of the sacrament of Holy Communion were said to become both materially and spiritually the body and blood of Christ, and the veneration of images with characteristic themes and motifs. The Baroque approach is markedly emotional: whereas the Ignatian forms of meditation of the sixteenth century had been rigorously intellectual (and continued to enjoy considerable popularity in the seventeenth century), the 'devout humanism' of St Francis de Sales with its emphasis upon the emotions grew increasingly popular during the Baroque period. De Sales popularised devotions such as those upon the wounds of Christ, the tears of the Magdalene and the ecstatic Teresa, and consequently the emphasis shifted from cerebral rigour to emotional intensity. Crashaw's favourite subjects illustrate this aspect of Counter-Reformation spirituality at work: the ecstasies and love wounds of St Teresa, Magdalene's tears, the sorrows of the Blessed Virgin Mary, the wounds and blood of the crucified Lord are all present in his poems.

Theologians and historians of Christian spirituality have not been, generally speaking, particularly sympathetic to Crashaw. One of the most critical, but not the most perceptive, has been Louis Bouyer whose hostile remarks are worth nothing as an example of this tendency:

All the tears, bitter potions, wings and flames . . . found in Herbert—the necessary apparatus of the poetic school stemming from John Donne—are to be found in Crashaw, but run to seed. His conceits are the most baroque liquefactions and incandesences of the whole of English literature. This High Church Anglican's *Saint Teresa* has often been compared to Bernini's. But the sort of clammy sensuality in which the erotic imagery is drenched is more embarassing in Crashaw if this be possible, and quickly leaves an after-taste of insipidity. It is the shamelessness of innocence, but an innocence that has passed maturity without ever reaching it. This falsely sensual liquor can only burn on a sea of sugariness... The psycho-analysts who detect a longing for the mother's breast behind Crashaw's orgy of pseudo-nuptial images are probably not far from the truth.*

This emotional concentration is accompanied by an element of surprise, as Crashaw usually treats these familiar subjects, such as the Crucifixion, from an unusual perspective reminiscent of the affected or excessive style associated with Mannerism (named from the Italian word *maniera*, meaning an impressive quality). The effect is partly to enhance the sense of dislocation in the reader and command his or her attention, as in 'Our Lord in his Circumcision to his Father', where the reader 'overhears' Christ addressing his Father; and partly to provide a basis for the reader to become emotionally involved in the subject of the poem.

In Crashaw's poetry the relation between world and spirit is both decisive and paradoxical: Crashaw reaches down into the senses for the emotional resources from which his poetry can create a spiritual ascent. In a popular prose treatise, *Marie Magdalens Funeral Teares* (1591) (one of the most popular themes of the Baroque period), the remarks of the English Jesuit poet Robert Southwell give some idea of how the emotional emphases of Baroque spirituality influenced Crashaw's writing:

> Passions I allow, and loves I approve, onely I would wishe that men would alter their object and better their intent. For passions being sequels of our nature, and allotted unto us as the handmaides of reason: there can be no doubt, but that as their author is good, and their end godly: so ther use tempered in the meane, implieth no offence.†

In this context the sensuous figure of the penitent Magdalene who washed Christ's feet with her tears, wiped them with her hair and anointed them with costly ointment, offers a vivid but contradictory image of how the world might be rightly perceived and used – if so 'tempered in the meane'. That the idea was a commonplace can be seen by its reflection in *Paradise Lost* where Milton has the archangel Michael provide instruction for the fallen Adam and Eve before their expulsion and advise them to observe 'the rule of not too much, by

* L. Bouyer, *A History of Christian Spirituality*, Vol. 3, p.13.
† Robert Southwell, *Marie Magdalens Funeral Teares*, London, 1591, Preface.

temperance taught . . .'.* That the point is precisely applicable to Crashaw's poetry is further illustrated by the preface to the 1646 edition of *Steps to the Temple* where we are told: *'So maist thou take a Poem hence, and tune thy soule by it, into a heavenly pitch; and thus refined and borne up upon the wings of meditation, in these Poems thou maist talke freely of God and of that other state.'*† Both metaphors, to temper 'in the meane' and to 'tune' one's soul, comprehend the emotions as a means of ascent to the spiritual and reflect the spirit of the devotional techniques of St Francis de Sales as they had been popularised by the Benedictine Augustine Baker (1575–1641). While Crashaw was independent of Baker, the latter's work demonstrates how Crashaw's writing reflected the spiritual fashions of the time, and how it employed the world of sense experience and the emotions rather than the intellect:

> And as for the exercise of *sensible Affections*, it belongs only to such soules as in their naturall temper are more tender and affectionate; whose love expresses it selfe with great *liquefaction* in sensible nature, so that they are easily moved to *teares*, and doe feele *warmth* and quick motions about the *heart*. . . Such *tender soules* as these, having withall a naturall good *propension to seeke God in their Interiour*, can easily exercise their affections to God in and by their corporall nature, without troubling themselves with seeking reasons and motives for it . . . ‡

A second point follows from this. Crashaw's spiritual ascent is characterised by a delight in the contradictory, the contraries which the Magdalene epitomises—as is suggested further by the epigraph he added in 1648:

> Loe where a WOUNDED HEART with Bleeding EYES conspire.
> Is she a FLAMING Fountain, or a Weeping fire!

Though paradox is universal in religious poetry and Metaphysical verse, here it is intensified as an emotional device which tunes the spirit to the eternal, and becomes an expression of what, in 'To The Name Above Every Name', he calls 'the witt of love'. This is most obvious in Crashaw's epigrams where he shows himself to be both a master of that form of rhetorical exercise, and, even more impressive, one who is able to give the epigram a very distinctive emotional forcefulness.

* John Milton, *Paradise Lost*, Book XI, line 533.
† L.C. Martin (ed.), *The Poems of Richard Crashaw*, p.75.
‡ Augustine Baker, *Sancta Sophia*, John Platte and Thomas Fievet, Douai, 1657, II, pp.139–40.

It is clear that the connections between spirituality and poetry in the period are a vital factor in any appreciation of Crashaw's work. A further illustration of the way in which his interests are part of a wider awareness is to see how closely they reflect those of his Puritan contemporary, John Milton. What the invocations in *Paradise Lost*, together with a range of allusions in various of Milton's poems, illustrate, is suggested—more modestly—in a minor poem of Crashaw's, 'To the Morning. Satisfaction for sleepe'. There is little evidence about how much Crashaw himself had achieved the mystical union of the contemplatives, but there is no doubt that he desired such a goal. Reminiscent of Milton in *Lycidas*, Crashaw shows here a determination that poetry shall be a spiritual aid, a means of vision which wings him to heaven to draw him back to earth, renewed:

> ...so my wakefull lay shall knocke
> At th' Orientall Gates; and duly mocke
> The early Larkes shrill Orizons to be
> An Anthem at the Dayes Nativitie.
> And the same rosie-fingered hand of thine,
> That shuts Nights dying eyes, shall open mine.

Baroque literary style

Apart from Crashaw, who writes as one whose imaginative stimulus came from outside England, the spirituality and art of the Counter-Reformation made little impact upon English poetry, and there is virtually nothing in English poetry before Crashaw that manifests the spirit of the Baroque in English literature. The exceptions to this are few: most notable is the poetry of Robert Southwell, a poet and Jesuit martyr who lived in Rome during the 1580s and experienced the beginnings of Baroque art, but who failed in his attempt to bring Italian poetic styles into English verse at the end of the sixteenth century. Another example is Giles Fletcher's lengthy, sensuous and slightly florid description of Christ's eyes in 'Christ's Victory and Triumph'.

The continental figure invariably cited as the decisive instance of the Baroque influence upon Crashaw is the poet Giambattista Marino (1569–1625) whose lush, sensuous and excessively elaborate style bears his name in the term consistently used to describe such writing—'Marinism'. That Crashaw both admired and was relatively intimate with Marino's work can be illustrated by his free and energetic translation of the first part of Marino's poem *La Strage de gli Innocenti.**

* 'Sospetto d'Herode'. Quoted in L.C. Martin (ed.), *The Poems of Richard Crashaw*, p.109.

Crashaw's style and development

It is difficult to speak of Crashaw's 'development' for several reasons, one of which is that his revisions of his works were minor and demonstrate an interest in additional elaboration rather than either honing or simplifying his style. His initial poems, as with those of many of his contemporaries, were more in the nature of exercises, and his initial dependence upon classical models for wit, especially Ovid, can be readily demonstrated. After this his lyrics steadily evolved towards longer narrative forms, and he moved from the use of the epigram and the closed couplet to the ode. The movement, then, was from a highly controlled form to one which appears relatively formless—where structure is largely dependent upon a careful use of rhyme patterns. This concern with elegant arrangements of sound and diction, variation of line lengths and stresses, and the adroit placing of unrhymed lines for maximum effect is an aspect of Baroque aesthetics. But Crashaw's practice goes beyond this: in his later works, through an increased use of various devices such as direct quotation and imperatives, the dramatic element is heightened to emphasise the consciousness of the poet.

This aspect of Crashaw's development is accompanied by the accumulation of clusters of images which, on the one hand, form part of the lush sensual surface embellishment that can distract the reader, but which, on the other, more substantially form part of a symbolic frame of reference through which he approaches his spiritual subject. Even a casual reading of such poems as 'To The Name Above Every Name' and 'The Flaming Heart' impresses the reader with the constant recurrence of sensory objects—flowers, precious stones, images of liquidity and abundance—to delineate qualities associated with the spiritual life.

His sensuous and sometimes grotesque figurative language is similarly part of the Baroque desire to express abstract, spiritual and figurative subjects in literal and tangible terms. When Crashaw writes in this manner, Marino's influence is most obvious: the danger is that when applied too literally to the paradoxes of Christian dogma, the effect of such a strong emphasis on the senses can be blasphemous. An instance of this is 'Prayer: An Ode', which, despite the biblical precedents for using erotic language to describe the relation to God of the soul, is for some tastes too reminiscent of a bedroom scene to illuminate the mystical union between God and the human soul that is the subject of the poem.

Nonetheless when Crashaw's literary development is seen in the context of his spiritual vision and distinctive spirituality, there are some remarkable successes. The accusations against Crashaw, either that his poems are formless or that his images are confused, are naive when it is realised that his aim is to suggest religious ecstasy. In short, in order to evoke an awareness of transcendence he deliberately stresses the emotions, goes beyond reason and logic, and blends sensations and categories.

Epigrams

Crashaw applied the devices of Ovidian wit to the traditional paradoxes of Christian faith. There was nothing especially innovative in this. Technically the method was familiar to Metaphysical wit: intellectual in its appeal, it endeavoured to contract a larger concept into an ingenious epigram. There were a number of Counter-Reformation exponents, such as the Jesuits Jacob Biedemann and Franciscus Remond, who used the epigram in relation to sacred subjects. These Jesuits employed the stylistic and verbal contractions and surprise turns that were appropriate to the epigram, but also evolved an elaborate and distinctive rhetoric that was heavily dependent upon paradoxes, puns and antitheses, and a common store of conceits and metaphors. Crashaw was able to call upon such examples.

Crashaw's Latin epigrams, *Epigrammata Sacra* (1634), are all on biblical texts, and most probably date from his academic exercises at Pembroke College when he had to write Latin and Greek verses on the scripture texts for every Sunday and feast day of the year. It is commonly acknowledged that these are some of the best Latin epigrams ever written by an Englishman, and those which he transposed into English display his sharp and playful intellect, as much as they may cause distaste by the occasional *grotesquerie* of their metaphors. For example, in the epigram upon Luke 11:27 with the text 'Blessed be the paps which thou hast sucked', Crashaw establishes a bizarre antithesis between Christ's painless suckling at Mary's breast and her need for spiritual nourishment through the blood flowing from the crucified Christ's side:

> Svppose he had been Tabled at thy Teates,
>   Thy hunger feeles not what he eates:
> Hee'l have his Teat e're long (a bloody one)
>   The Mother then must suck the Son.

Among the most striking of the divine epigrams is that on Matthew 27:12 'And he answered them nothing'. The witty play upon the concept of 'nothing' is almost worthy of Donne, but its distinctiveness from Donne's epigrams lies in its primary emotional thrust being outward towards the object of devotion and not inward either to complement the poet's wit or voice his questions:

O Mighty *Nothing*! unto thee
Nothing, wee owe all things that bee.
God spake once when hee all things made,
Hee sav'd all when hee *Nothing* said.
The world was made of *Nothing* then;
'Tis made by *Nothyng* now againe.

The witty—and serious—possibilities of this concept recur in the other poems which, though longer than the epigram, retain many of its characteristics, including the closed couplet. A good example from *The Delights of the Muses* is that 'Upon Mr Staininough's Death'.

Secular poems

Written mainly in a couplet form, *The Delights of the Muses* (1646) is primarily a collection of translations, compliments and elegies of minor interest. Most merely show Crashaw as a talented poet, but occasionally illustrate his propinquity to the 'School of Donne'. 'Loves Horoscope' is an obvious example where Crashaw playfully explores the conventional contradictions of human love. Intellectual in its structure, it lacks the incisiveness of Donne's wit and the dramatic surprise and twist he can bring to his conceits, though it demonstrates something of the interest in contraries which is so central to Crashaw's religious poetry.

Two poems, however, those which open and close the collection, stand aside as being of considerable merit in themselves and among the best of Crashaw's work. The final poem in the collection, 'Wishes to his (supposed) Mistresse', had appeared in a shorter form in a collection in 1641 and can be distinguished from the others in *The Delights of the Muses* by its cultivated Jonsonian simplicity of manner and its celebration of natural virtues. The subject is again that of love but here, though spiced with Caroline wit, it is restrained and balanced by 'A well tam'd Heart', and developed and enriched through an appreciation of what is natural—for instance, pleasant human companionship and conversation. In contrast to Jonson, however, the subject is purely speculative: Crashaw creates an ideal—'That not impossible shee/ That shall command my heart and mee'—and the realisation of his affections remains a spiritual aspiration, as the epigram 'On Marriage' in the middle of the collection suggests:

I would be married, but I'de have no Wife,
I would be married to a single Life.

More substantial in its achievement is the lengthy opening poem, 'Musicks Duell'. In this much admired work Crashaw provides a vigorous free translation of a Latin poem by the Jesuit Famianus Strada (1572–1649) which had been often emulated by other English poets, including some of Crashaw's contemporaries. As so often happens in his translations, Crashaw goes beyond a passive role and re-creates the poem to about three times the length of Strada's fifty-eight lines. In itself, the formal subject of the poem, a supposed contest between a nightingale and a poet, or singers or musicians, was common enough in seventeenth-century writing. What is remarkable about Crashaw's translation is his control over the couplet form and his tendency to favour language luxuriant with sensual imagery (a feature which the divine poems develop further). Thus we find such words as 'lubricke', 'trembling', 'sugred', 'liquid', 'creame', 'sweet-lipp'd', 'soft Bosome', and the nightingale's song is described as issuing from:

> . . . out of her Breast
> That ever-bubling spring; the sugred Nest
> Of her delicious soule, that there does lye
> Bathing in streames of liquid Melodie . . .

The similarity with the divine poems is quite deliberate. For where in the divine poems Crashaw aims at suggesting religious ecstasy, here too he is concerned with ecstasy. This is clearly shown further on (lines 102–4):

> Her little soule is ravisht: and so pour'd
> Into loose extasies, that shee is plac't
> Above her self, Musicks *Enthusiast.*

To complement this there is the occasional confusion of images—as in lines 125–6—where sweetness, breath and softness are combined in defiance of logic and syntax. As in the divine poems, this evokes the sense of a spiritual rapture in terms of sensual experience.

The subject of the poem demands Crashaw's knowledge of music and his skill in imitating a sense of musical sound by onomatopoeia, smooth syntax, repetitions and liquid vowels. While the lutanist triumphs through his capacity to produce harmony—the finite analogue of the music of the spheres and the ordering principle of the universe—the thrust of the poem is towards a new type of perception, the experience of rapture. The structural climactic development is impressive, as Crashaw makes the metre and syntax falter so as to suggest the collapse of sense and reason under the pressure of ecstatic experience. Reminiscent of the mystical 'death' of religious experience, the nightingale's ecstasy culminates in death—'so sweet a Grave!'

Steps to The Temple

The first edition of *Steps to The Temple* (1646) is of particular interest
because it shows the early form of poems which were considerably
revised in the subsequent editions of 1648 and 1652; and the list of
contents shows how the work was neatly divided into the sequence of
religious poems—which began with 'The Weeper' and closed with the
poem 'On Hope' in answer to Cowley—and the 'secular' poems mentioned above. The second edition of 1648 is considerably larger,
though not so attractively printed, and includes versions of 'The Office
of the Holy Ghost' and rather florid translations and ornamentations
of several medieval hymns. The line of development apparent here is
completed in *Carmen Deo Nostro* where most of the poems are repub-
lished with some particularly important additions.

Carmen Deo Nostro

This is certainly the most notable edition of Crashaw's poems. When it
was published in 1652 Crashaw had been dead for about three years, so
responsibility for the arrangement of the poems may not have been his
but that of Thomas Car who oversaw its publication. However, the
general shape of the work appears so coherent that it is most likely to
have been designed by Crashaw, rather than being an ingenious arrangement imposed by an 'editor'.

The overall design is determined by Crashaw's conversion: the liturgy and devotional life of Roman Catholicism dominates. While Herbert had generally followed the shape of the Christian year in *The
Temple*, Crashaw begins his collection with a dedicatory poem that sets
the mood and urges his friend the Countess of Denbigh to convert to
Rome. Beyond this the use of emblems to fuse visual art and devotion
is typical of the spirit of Counter-Reformation devotion. Thomas
Car's prefatory epigram clearly demonstrates this:

> This to the eare speakes wonders; that will trye
> To speake the same, yet lowder, to the eye.
> Both their aymes are holy, both conspire
> To wound, to burn the hart with heauenly fire. (lines 10−13)*

Car's claim in the epigraph to the epigram that 'the pictures in the
following Poemes ...the Author first made with his owne hand'
implies that Crashaw engraved all the illustrations. This has been
questioned, in view of their varying style and quality, but the two
accompanying the poems 'The Weeper' and the dedicatory poem, 'To
The Countess of Denbigh', are most likely to be Crashaw's own.

* Quoted in L.C. Martin (ed.), *The Poems of Richard Crashaw*, p.235.

The sequence of poems then follows the cycle of the feast days of the liturgical year: 'To The Name Above Every Other Name' anticipates the themes of Advent and leads naturally to the Christmastide poems which are followed by 'The Office of the Holy Cross' and a series of hymns and epigrams on the Passion and Crucifixion. Since the Eucharist is considered the fruit of the Passion, it is a logical progression from poems on the Passion to translations of Aquinas's two Eucharistic hymns, and this sequence is completed by a meditation on the Day of Judgement. The feast days of saints provide another development which begins with two poems on the Virgin Mary, the poem 'The Weeper' and a small sequence of the important 'Teresa' poems. Finally, standing apart from the liturgical focus is a group of poems concerned with various aspects of Christian living which include the 'Description of a Religious House' and the—radically changed—poems of the Cowley-Crashaw debate on 'hope' with their spirited affirmation of hope as an anticipation of eternal life.

'To The Countess of Denbigh'

Both Crashaw's religious enthusiasm and his closeness to the Metaphysical school are most obvious in this dedicatory poem, 'To the Noblest & best of Ladyes', with its emblem and verse of the locked heart. Remarkable amongst Crashaw's works for its dearth of sensuous language and its combination of a dramatic opening with an abstract vocabulary, it provides an accomplished expression of the state of spiritual irresolution in eight-syllabled couplets:

What heau'n-intreated HEART is This?
Stands trembling at the gate of blisse;
Holds fast the door, yet dares not venture
Fairly to open it, and enter.
Whose DEFINITION is a doubt
Twixt life & death, twixt in & out . . .
Ah linger not, lou'd soul! a slow
And late consent was a long no . . .

Crashaw here shows a curiosity as to what motivates the heart in this situation: 'What magick bolts, what mystick Barres/ Maintain the will in these strange warres!' The answer is provided in the verse accompanying the emblem of the locked heart, ''Tis loue alone can hearts unlock', and the poem gains momentum from line 27 to the end where, using some conventions of secular love poetry—in particular the idea of the dart of love and the impatient urging of the woman to yield before it is too late—he urges divine love to unlock 'the self-shutt cabinet of an vnsearcht soul.'

Hymns

While Crashaw's musical skill in 'Musicks Duell' places him alongside
Vaughan and Herbert, the numerous hymns in his work show how
strongly he was influenced by music and forms of vocal devotion and
the liturgy itself. His free translations of Latin plainsong texts lack the
spirit of the originals and provide instead a warm emotional approach
to their subject.

'To The Name Above Every Name, The Name of Jesus' recalls the
ancient 'Scala Meditatoria' of Mauburnus (?1460–?1501), as Crashaw
rationally expresses the various stages in the development of the poem
and uses sensual imagery in a wholly non-material or symbolic way to
make of the name of Jesus 'An vniuersall SYNOD of All sweets'. He
begins with an invocation of the saints to assist in his act of praise, and
then turns to nature, the music of the spheres and art itself to achieve a
crescendo of 'All-imbracing SONG'.

Crashaw's craftsman-like variation of line length, using the longer
lines for more elaborate sensual imagery and the shorter lines for more
striking emphasis, allows him to achieve some striking effects of wit.
So, for example, he playfully imagines the universal synod pronounc-
ing a dogma:

> An vniuersall SYNOD of All sweets;
> By whom it is defined Thus
> > That no Perfume
> > For euer shall presume
> To passe for Odoriferous,
> But such alone whose sacred Pedigree
> Can proue it Self some kin (sweet name) to Thee.

There is a tendency to overload the senses with rich imagery, however,
and this can produce some inappropriate effects, such as the
description of martyrs' wounds as 'Fair purple Doores, of love's
devising'. Nevertheless, this does demonstrate the unabashed emotional thrust which is the essence of Crashaw's style.

The hymn, 'In The Holy Nativity of Our Lord God: A Hymn Sung
as by the Shepheards', addresses a witty problem, that of finding a
resting place for the infant Christ, but it also employs imagery drawn
from Cavalier love lyrics together with the tradition of pastoral
dialogue familiar from courtly entertainments, such as the masque
with the antiphonal exchanges sung by the shepherds and a full chorus.
It is typical that the stress is upon the theme of love, and the opening
motif is drawn from the tradition of a lover's dawn-song (one famous
example being that of Sir William Davenant's (1606–68) 'The lark now

leaves his watry nest'. While the language generally produces a sense of cloying sweetness, there are some acute asides such as the description of 'slippery soules in smiling eyes', and Crashaw manages to combine sweetness with the paradoxes of the Christian faith to evoke a sense of strong devotion—particularly in the opening lines of the chorus:

Wellcome, all WONDERS in one sight!
  Æternity shutt in a span.
Sommer in Winter. Day in Night.
  Heauen in earth, & GOD in MAN.
Great little one! whose all-embracing birth
Lifts earth to heauen, stoopes heau'n to earth.

'The Weeper'

'The Weeper' has come in for considerable criticism from critics who find that its imagery is excessive and unrestrained and, in particular, that Crashaw's approach in this poem is too emotional. Whereas Donne's imagery is often excessive, his intellectual stance prevents the reader being embarrassed. Not so with Crashaw.

The aim of the poem should be clearly understood. Its object, revealed in the last line, is to promote a proper devotion—devotion to Christ. The logical structure to promote this is based upon emotional consistency rather than reason, and moves from heaven to earth, and from the historic person of Mary Magdalene to her influence as a spiritual principle.

The conceits and images may grate upon a modern reader, but they nonetheless follow a devotional logic which is based upon the view that the spiritual world can be comprehended through direct analogies with the things of the earth, and that, properly directed, the soul may thereby ascend to God. Bizarre though it appears to talk of the Magdalene's tears as 'cream', nonetheless they are spiritually 'nourishing' because her involuntary weeping springs from her exemplary love of God. Indeed, even the general thrust of the language, which is obviously meant to celebrate Magdalene as an example of spiritual grace and abundance, is based upon Crashaw's elaboration of biblical texts and imagery: for example, the well known complaint of the Apostles, that she had wasted a precious jar of ointment, lies behind the cluster of conceits which celebrate her as a 'wandering mine / A voluntary mint'.

The Teresa poems

Loue, thou art Absolute sole lord
OF LIFE & DEATH . . .

These measured and assured tones characterise the various poems in honour of St Teresa which are certainly amongst the most satisfying of Crashaw's works. Written in unostentatious octosyllabic couplets, 'A Hymn to the Name and Honour of St Teresa' has Crashaw's typical emphasis upon the nature and power of Christian love—''Tis LOVE not YEARES or LIMBS that can/ Make the Martyr, or the man'—and the poet approaches his subject directly, with few conceits, and achieves a remarkable fusion of manner, mood and theme.

Teresa serves Crashaw as a model for his understanding of the spiritual life. The common religious paradoxes are treated with a devout wittiness which never detracts from the seriousness of the subject and which saves the poem from excessive sweetness. Crashaw's interest in martyrdom, and his high regard for it, contrasts sharply with Donne's scepticism:

> O how oft shalt thou complain
> Of a sweet & subtle PAIN.
> Of intolerable IOYES;
> Of a DEATH, in which who dyes
> Loues his death, and dyes again . . .

The point of the poem is its transformation of the idea of martyrdom. It suggests that God has denied Teresa physical martyrdom so that she may demonstrate that love is also 'absolute sole lord of life', and her 'martyrdom' will be to live and to endure the spiritual rigours of the contemplative life. The idea of the transformation of the soul, 'like a soft lump of incense, hasted/ By too hott a fire', by love or its processes—which include martyrdom – and the constant play upon 'love' and 'dye', dominates the poem. As with the Magdalene, Teresa's devotion leads her to:

> . . . walk with HIM those wayes of light
> Which who in death would liue to see,
> Must learn in life to dy like thee.

The other Teresa poems are similar in kind. The closing lines of 'The Flaming Heart' are particularly fine, for there Crashaw appears to disclose his own longing for an experience of religious ecstasy—something of which may also be hinted at by his allusion to Dionysius the Areopagite and the mystical *via negativa* (which taught that the ascent of the soul to God must be in 'darkness' and without reliance upon the light of the intellect) in the hymn 'In the Glorious Epiphanie'. Having used various witty paradoxes and antitheses earlier in the poem, he finally transcends them in vivid burning exclamations:

> O thou vndanted daughter of desires!
> By all thy dowr of LIGHTS & FIRES;

By all the eagle in thee, all the doue;
By all thy liues & deaths of loue;
By thy larg draughts of intellectuall day,
And by thy thirsts of loue more large than they;
By all thy brim-fill'd Bowles of feirce desire
By thy last Morning's draught of liquid fire;
By the full kingdome of that finall kisse
That seiz'd thy parting Soul, & seal'd thee his;
By all the heau'ns thou hast in him
(Fair sister of the SERAPHIM!
By all of HIM we have in THEE;
Leaue nothing of my SELF in me.
Let me so read thy life, that I
Vnto all life of mine may dy.

Chapter 7

Henry Vaughan

Happy those early dayes! when I
Shin'd in my Angell-infancy.
Before I understood this place
Appointed for my second race,
Or taught my soul to fancy ought
But a white, Celestiall thought,
When yet I had not walkt above
A mile, or two, from my first love,
And looking back (at that short space,)
Could see a glimpse of his bright-face;
When on some *gilded Cloud*, or *flowre*
My gazing soul would dwell an houre,
And in those weaker glories spy
Some shadows of eternity . . . ('The Retreate')*

The lyrical ease and elegant simplicity of these lines capture the
popular image of Henry Vaughan (1622–95) as he is regarded today:
the tone so evocative of innocence, the sense of a vision which
transforms the mundane appearances of daily life—all these are here.
Indeed, it has often been pointed out that the sentiment of these lines is
reminiscent of Wordsworth's 'Intimations of Immortality'. The
comparison is understandable, for on the surface both poems seem to
demonstrate a kind of nature mysticism. Yet, while Vaughan
approaches natural phenomena with a sense of reverence and wonder
similar to Wordsworth's lofty exclamations, the difference between
the two poets is immense. Vaughan's approach to nature is not that of
a Romanticist. For one thing his tone is quite different: it is far more
sober. This is by no means incidental, for his subject matter is specifically religious and his view of nature is dictated by religious considera-
tions. In Wordsworth, nature may be a substitute for God; in
Vaughan, on the other hand, nature is seen as a testimony to God its
creator.

* Quoted in French Fogle (ed.), *The Complete Poetry of Henry Vaughan*, Doubleday,
New York, 1964, pp.169–71. Unless otherwise indicated, all quotations from Vaughan's
works are from this edition.

Life

Unfortunately we know much less about Vaughan's long life than we do about his contemporaries, Herbert and Crashaw. We know that he was born in Breconshire, Wales, to an ancient family of modest means and that, together with his twin brother Thomas (who later became a famous Hermetic philosopher), he was educated first by Matthew Herbert, a schoolmaster and clergyman at Llangattock, and then at Jesus College, Oxford from 1638 to 1640. After Oxford Vaughan went on to study law in London at the Inns of Court where he felt the literary influence of such 'sons' of Ben Jonson as Randolph (1605–35), Cartwright (1611–43), Cleveland, Davenant, Habington (1605–64) and Carew, but his career was interrupted by the Civil War and he returned to Wales in 1642 to serve briefly on the Royalist side. Some of his poems, such as 'An Elegie on the death of Mr R.W ...' * and 'The King Disguis'd' which refers to Charles I's escape from Oxford in 1646, hint at this aspect of his life, and there is no doubt that he disliked Puritanism and favoured the religious disposition of the Anglican Church—that moderate form of Calvinism which Herbert adorned. The latter poem also glances mournfully at the wreckage wrought by the religious zeal of the Puritans and compares it to the king's unhappy situation: 'Like some fair Church, which Zeal to Charcoals burn'd,/ Or his own Court now to an Ale-house turn'd.'†

It appears that Vaughan married twice. His first wife was Catherine Wise, whom he married about 1646, and, after Catherine's death, he married her sister Elizabeth—in about 1655. Although there is no record of Vaughan having any medical qualifications, in a letter to John Aubrey (15 June 1673) he mentions that at Usk he had 'practised [physic] now for many years with good success'‡, where, in addition to his poetry and devotional works, he translated and wrote a number of medical and alchemical works—and a reader should notice the extent to which medical imagery dominates his preface to *Silex Scintillans* (1655).

Influences

Place and family may account for some notable elements of Vaughan's work. His identification with the traditions of his native Wales can be seen in his adoption of the title 'The Silurist', a title which alludes to that part of south-east Wales formerly inhabited by an ancient tribe of Britons, the Silures. Fully bilingual, Vaughan was able to bring to

* See particularly, lines 50–5.
† 'The King Disguis'd', lines 31–2.
‡ Quoted in French Fogle (ed.), *The Complete Poetry of Henry Vaughan*, p.xvi.

English poetry such characteristics of Welsh speech as the extensive use of alliteration, assonance and consonance rhymes, the Welsh *dyfalu* (the animated multiplication of comparisons and similes), extensive use of *s/z* rhymes, and the attribution of gender to non-personified nouns. While the tradition of the *dyfalu* involved nature as the frame of reference for its metaphors, the references to nature which abound in Vaughan's poetry are more than a reflection of a literary tradition and suggest his acute awareness of and sensitivity to the Welsh countryside around Usk. No other Metaphysical poet, not even Herbert, watches earth and water, sky and birds with such passion and delicacy.

Quite what influence Vaughan's family had on his work is uncertain. Certainly the effect of William Vaughan's death in 1648 was considerable, but the most substantial family influence appears to have been that of his twin brother Thomas, through whom we can assume Vaughan made contact with Hermetic philosophy, its literature and essential ideas. Hermeticism was an esoteric medieval science involving elements of alchemy and magic. Studied closely by such Renaissance scholars as Copernicus, it took its name from Hermes Trismegistus, the supposed author of the *Hermetica* (and other works), a book which addressed the concept of a cosmic religion. A variety of ideas were spawned under the name of Hermeticism: probably the most consistent of these was the philosophical notion that there were only three chemical principles, which were salt, sulphur and mercury, and that all natural phenomena could be explained by them. The extent to which Hermetic ideas influenced Vaughan's work is difficult to assess, since its basic approach to the world and many of its concepts conflict with the essentials of Vaughan's profound Christian faith. Nonetheless, in common with other Renaissance thinkers, he was able to draw upon a variety of eclectic and apparently contradictory sources, whether Hermetic, Neoplatonic or alchemical, and use them as the basis for the rich thought, glowing vocabulary and vital natural images through which he expressed his Christian vision.

Vaughan's religious sensibility is a decisive factor in his writing, though it is tied to historical circumstances. As was the case with Herbert, Vaughan was, on the one hand, influenced by the theology of Calvin, and, on the other, by that of St Augustine, who, after St Paul, was probably the most influential Christian theologian and of particular importance for the Reformers during the Protestant Reformation. Vaughan's acceptance of the doctrines to which this theology might have bound him—in particular those of the Fall, the depravity of the will and belief in predestination—was, however, tempered by a deeply personal sense of the immanence, or presence, of God in the whole of creation. His devotional life appears to have lacked Herbert's deep interest in the people, the traditions and the worship of the Church, the intimacy with Christ as a friend and the Church as a community in history. But Herbert was writing when the position of the Anglican Church was not in doubt. This was not so with Vaughan, who wrote after Parliament had forbidden Anglican worship. Denied the institutional foundation of Anglicanism, he concentrated upon an individual spirituality which occasionally touched upon mystical awareness, and he also viewed nature as though it were a book full of signs that pointed to the presence of God, a belief to which the doctrines of the Creation as the work of God, and the doctrine of the Incarnation as showing God's presence in human flesh, gave strong support. In this, Vaughan has some points of similarity with Marvell, for while his poetic and religious sensibilities are quite distinct from Marvell's, his use of the pastoral as a sacred allegory and nature as a means of spiritual ascent is similar.

Almost of equal weight as determining factors in Vaughan's writing are the two great influences of George Herbert and the Bible itself. Herbert's influence is directly testified to by Vaughan in the preface to the 1655 edition of *Silex Scintillans* where he identifies himself with the many 'pious *Converts*' gained by Herbert's 'holy *life* and *verse*'. Indirectly, Herbert's influence is obvious in the extensive borrowings of titles, lines, phrases and imitations of stanzaic forms. Such borrowings were common at the time, but Vaughan's is the most substantial example of one poet's reliance upon another. This 'dependence', however, was not passive. Although Herbert initiated Vaughan into religious poetry, in numerous instances Vaughan impresses his own mark on a borrowing, and, in his best later work, achieves a new range of poetic experience. In short, 'Herbert may have made Vaughan a poet, but he did not make him in his own image.'*

Like Herbert, Vaughan was influenced by the language and images of the Bible, and, like Herbert and also Bunyan, he commonly treats biblical places and spiritual qualities within an allegorical structure, with the effect that he evokes a sense of universal Christian experience. Thus from the common stock of biblical allusions, sources and subjects, he generates a language that carries a range of original and resonant overtones with symbolic values. Christian symbolism has been honed over centuries of exegesis, and, to quote a theologian, 'the symbol participates in the reality of that for which it stands'.† The truth of this observation is most apparent in Vaughan's symbolic portrayal of the landscape, for here he uses the biblical account of Eden as a source for symbol and metaphor in an impressive manner. In this context it is worthwhile considering the biblical account of Eden in some

* Joan Bennett, *Five Metaphysical Poets*, Cambridge University Press, Cambridge, 1964, p.85.
† Paul Tillich, *Systematic Theology*, James Nisbet & Co, London, 1968, Vol. 1, p.265.

detail. In the original Hebrew, Eden (which means pleasure) was the name given to the garden created by God. The story is found in the book of Genesis which includes the account of the making of the world, and of the first man and woman, Adam and Eve, who inhabited the Garden. The Renaissance reader believed this earthly paradise actually to have existed, and used it as a symbol of perfection and sinlessness. Comparisons were made with the idea of a 'Golden Age' in classical literature (mentioned by Hesiod (c.800BC), or the Garden of the Hesperides from which Hercules had to steal the Golden Apples.

Another image, less generally used but still of immense importance for the religious poets, was the Feast of Pentecost, the festival in which the Christian Church celebrates the descent of the Holy Spirit, said to be accompanied by a rushing wind and tongues of fire. The Sunday on which this is remembered is also commonly known as 'Whit Sunday'. An instance of both these religious images being used in one poem is in 'Regeneration' where spiritual experience is expressed through Vaughan's fusion of Edenic and Pentecostal symbolism:

> It was a bank of flowers, where I descried
>   (Though 'twas mid-day,)
> Some fast asleepe, others broad-eyed
>   And taking in the Ray,
>   Here musing long, I heard
>   A rushing wind
> Which still increas'd, but whence it stirr'd,
>   No where I could not find . . .

Style and development

Vaughan's development as a poet begins with his collections *Poems, with the tenth Satyre of Juvenal* (1646) and *Olor Iscanus* ('Swan of Usk', published in 1651). Written mainly in the elegant Cavalier style, these poems are characterised by their lack of conviction and suggest the work of a man of literary taste but no particular talent who was open to various influences but without a strong motivating centre. They mark Vaughan as a follower of Ben Jonson, whom he both celebrates in the first poem and then emulates in those other poems which deal with the themes of friendship and retirement which are typical of the royalist verse of the period.

In various lines and conceits Donne's influence may also be detected: sometimes directly, sometimes through one of Donne's numerous imitators such as Habington or Carew. While 'To Amoret, of the difference 'twixt him, and other Lovers, and what true Love is' copies the Metaphysical conceit in Donne's 'The Ecstasie' and 'Air and Angels', it uses nature with more conviction than Donne. On the other hand, his conceit of the loadstones to describe the relations of the lovers lacks both conviction and, most of all, Donne's incisiveness. The witty environment of London figures in 'A Rhapsodie', but again it demonstrates his emulation of a literary fashion rather than displaying the cutting edge of genuine 'wit'.

A marked change occurs in *Silex Scintillans*. In the preface to the 1655 edition Vaughan disparages his previous work and its literary milieu. In his rejection of the decadent witty style he apologises for his own *'greatest follies'* and deplores both love poetry, which is a 'wallowing in *impure thoughts* and *scurrilous conceits*', and decadent religious poetry where writers 'dash *Scriptures*, and the *sacred Relatives of God* with their impious conceits'. He praises Herbert for his influence against this diseased literary fashion and for being 'the first, that with any effectual success attempted a *diversion* of this foul and overflowing *stream*...and gave the first check to a most flourishing and admired *wit* of his time.'* Though Donne and Herrick have both been suggested as the 'wit' so unfavourably mentioned, certain identification is impossible.

Not only does *Silex Scintillans* mark a new sense of direction in Vaughan's work, but it also indicates a new sense of some personal centre which drew together his life and his work. The emblem which introduces *Silex* hints at the depth and power of Vaughan's feeling and experience: it is an engraving of a stony heart being struck by the fire of God, and it both comments upon the title of the work ('sparkling flint') and suggests its didactic purpose.

Although the preface is very slight so far as poetic theory is concerned, Vaughan's purpose is clear from the outset: he testifies to the effect of Herbert's poetry upon him and his own status as one of Herbert's 'converts'. Some points emerge from this. First, that Herbert's influence and poetry assisted Vaughan's realisation of what he wanted to write and provided a model for its achievement. Second, the connection between Herbert's life and his poetry suggested the dedicated life as the key to sacred poetry. The idea has had some notable exponents, perhaps the most impressive being Milton, who declared that 'he who would not be frustrate of his hope to write well hereafter in laudable things, ought himself to be a true poem.'† Vaughan's argument in his preface is reminiscent of Milton: having attacked unchaste authors—as Milton did—and proclaimed himself in favour of 'sublime and pure thoughts', he likewise declares that he who would write 'A *true Hymn*' must 'strive (by all means) for *perfection* and true *holyness*.'‡

* Quoted in French Fogle (ed.), *The Complete Poetry of Henry Vaughan* pp.259 – 60.
†John Milton, *An Apology Against a Pamphlet Called 'A Modest Confutation of the Animadversions upon the Remonstrant Against Smectymnuus'*, 1642.
‡ Quoted in French Fogle (ed.), *The Complete Poetry of Henry Vaughan*, p.260.

The simplicity of Vaughan's language is a point of contrast between him and the Metaphysical tradition from which he proceeds. In *Silex Scintillans* his focus upon a world of spiritual reality issues from a sacramental vision which finds expression in homely language and natural images. The fireworks of Donnean wit are out of place here, and there are fewer puns, ambiguities and conceits than in Herbert. In the tradition both of Christian interpretation and poetry upon sacred themes, religious images and figures, or 'types', provide the basis which underpins the poems and their central image clusters. These image clusters include the elemental contrast of light and darkness, the vitality of life and nature, and the sense of divine grace which is expressed through various images of coolness and moisture. On the one hand, this use of religious models places individual experience in the context of biblical examples and precedents. See, for instance, Vaughan's remarks in 'White Sunday':

Besides, thy method with thy own,
Thy own dear people pens our times,
Our stories are in theirs set down
And penalties spread to our Crimes.

On the other hand, the symbolic resonances of the various image clusters have the tendency to universalise spiritual experience as, for example, in the contrast between light and darkness which evokes a sense of exploration through the natural world leading towards spiritual illumination.

Not only is Vaughan's language simpler than that of Donne or Herbert, but the principles of organisation and structure within his poems reflect a different purpose. He is not concerned with the taut intellectual analysis of a spiritual state, but rather with the expression of emotions within the spiritual life. The point can be demonstrated by comparing Herbert's 'Church-monuments' with Vaughan's 'The World'. Vaughan's poem opens dramatically—'I saw Eternity the other night'—and then proceeds to a discursive and emotional comparison of worldly obsessions with the life of eternity. Whereas in Herbert's intensely cerebral organisation the essential idea or conclusion does not emerge until the poem has been worked through, and its full impact felt only when the last line is reached, in Vaughan the essential contrast is contained in the first stanza. The subsequent stanzas do not clarify the thought, but merely expand its emotional force:

I saw Eternity the other night
Like a great *Ring* of pure and endless light,
   All calm, as it was bright,

And round beneath it, Time in hours, days, years
    Driv'n by the spheres
Like a vast shadow mov'd, In which the world
    And all her train were hurl'd;
The doting lover in his queintest strain
    Did there Complain,
Neer him, his Lute, his fancy, and his flights,
    Wit sours delights,
With gloves, and knots the silly snares of pleasure
    Yet his dear Treasure
All scatter'd lay, while he his eys did pour
    Upon a flowr.

Whereas in his secular poems Vaughan tends to favour the rhymed couplet, his religious poetry has far greater stanzaic variety. In some instances he adopts some of Herbert's verse forms but without attaining his musical and experimental achievements. Examples of his borrowings in versification include dialogue poems such as 'Resurrection and Immortality'; a poem with some features of the hieroglyph or emblem, 'The Wreath'; and songs introduced by a poem in a different metre, such as 'Palm Sunday' or 'The Search'. Vaughan varies stanza and line lengths but, unlike Herbert, his strength lies in a long and loose line and stanza pattern. 'The Waterfall' is a fine example of his ability to realise variety within a regular structure through a play upon the variations of cadence achieved through the use of mid-line pauses and enjambment. In fact, the visual impression of the printed poem suggests the appearance of the waterfall itself—the movements are now 'flowing' and then 'falling'.

Vaughan and the art of meditation

By comparison with what we know about Herbert or Donne, our ignorance of Vaughan's life and spiritual interests is baffling. He did, however, leave one remarkable insight into his spiritual life and methods, the devotional work *The Mount of Olives* (1652). The title of this work provides Vaughan with a key symbol for the spiritual life, and it is consistently used as such in his poems. As with many primers of this sort that were published during the period, Vaughan's work provides a series of devotions for use throughout the day and upon a variety of occasions: so there are prayers for waking and on going to sleep, a few meditations, and a series of private ejaculations for the user to make on specific instances—such as on hearing a clock chime. The general purpose is to bind prayer intimately into daily life.

The connection between *The Mount of Olives* and Vaughan's poetry is close. First, both issue from an integrated vision of life. As with the poems, *The Mount of Olives* displays how Vaughan's devotional life and situation reflect the political and social uncertainty of the period and the religious aspects of that uncertainty. The sober emphasis of his preface upon simple devotion contrasts with the wild excesses and millenialism (the belief that the kingdom of Christ was about to be established on earth) of some of the Puritan factions in the 1650s: *'I onely wish them real, and that their actions did not tell the world, they are rapt into some other place.'* Second, the poems are written for the spiritually minded reader who will also be interested in the devotions. Vaughan excuses himself from writing *'a large discourse of Devotion'* with the comment that *'thou hast them already as briefly delivered as possibly I could, in my* Sacred Poems.' Both works, then, are written for the reader who is a practitioner in devotion and who has already embarked upon a spiritual journey in the course of which, despite the prohibitions levied against the Anglican Church by Parliament under the Commonwealth, he is shown to be in company with other souls. Vaughan's terms echo the opening poem 'Regeneration' and its engagement with the world: *'Think not that thou art alone upon this Hill, there is an innumerable company both before and behinde thee. Those with their Palms in their hands, and those expecting them. If therefore the dust of this world chance to prick thine eyes, suffer it not to blinde them . . .'.*

In short, the significance of *The Mount of Olives* for the reader of Vaughan's poetry lies in part in the reminder it provides of the intimate connection between Vaughan's devotion and his poetry; and for the points at which it shows his familiarity with the various devotional modes and how he may have had recourse to them in his sacred poems. The emphasis is practical, not theoretical. While there are examples of meditation by similitude and by biblical analogy, Vaughan's caution, practicality and reserve suggest his experience in matters of spiritual discipline and instruction. They suggest, too, that he reserved some of the more difficult things for his poetry where, as in the preface to *Silex Scintillans* (1655), he observes 'you will (peradventure) observe some *passages*, whose *history* or *reason* may seem something *remote.'*

Silex Scintillans

Although written and published in two parts (1650/55), the obvious comparison for *Silex Scintillans* is Herbert's *The Temple*. Both works appear to have been planned as aesthetic and devotional entities. Vaughan's whole work is presented within the framework of a spiritual journey toward illumination—as, for example, in 'The Search' and 'The Pilgrimage'; but it is a journey through the wilderness, for which experience he draws upon the Christian models provided by the Old Testament figure of Ishmael in 'Begging (II)', 'Providence' and 'The Seed growing secretly'.

'Regeneration', the first poem in the first collection, establishes the general mood and tone of Part I, its subject being the poet's experience of 'conversion'. Other poems build upon this basic experience and its consequences, such as various spiritual states and early stages of spiritual awareness and anxiety. The most striking of these are probably 'The Search' and 'Vanity of Spirit', but the titles of some others suggest their common tenor—for example, 'Misery', 'The Relapse', 'Distraction', 'Unprofitablenes', and so on. Another group of poems recall *The Temple* by their treatment of various Church feast days and the sacraments, or their use of biblical events as models—as in *'Isaacs Marriage'*.

Part II is pervaded by a distinctive tone of spiritual assurance which contrasts sharply with the spiritual uncertainty of Part I. Though the preface now adds an extra dimension, the tone is again set by the poem which opens the collection. 'Ascension-day' uses the example of Christ's Ascension to suggest spiritual progression and aspiration—'I soar and rise/ Up to the skies,/Leaving the world their day'—and to suggest a shift of focus from the material world to that of spiritual reality. From pained nostalgia for the lost earthly paradise, Vaughan's thought moves toward joyful anticipation of the new and heavenly Jerusalem of the Book of Revelation. The connection between the two collections in *Silex Scintillans* can be seen in the way that not only is there a complementary direction of focus, but some poems in Part II are counterparts of those in Part I—for example, 'They are all gone into the world of light!' supplements the views of 'The World' from Part I. There are, however, fewer poems on ecclesiastical occasions in Part II and more on nature as a means of spiritual revelation for the individual; while the final few poems focus on the end of the world and the transformation of all things by God. This focus is combined with a sense of imminent death on the poet's part—as in 'L'Envoy' where creation is transparent with the glory of God and Vaughan composes himself to wait with patience 'Till all be ready'.

'Regeneration'

A Ward, and still in bonds, one day
    I stole abroad,
It was high-spring, and all the way
    Primros'd, and hung with shade;
    Yet, was it frost within,
      And surly winds

Blasted my infant buds, and sinne
Like Clouds ecclips'd my mind.

These opening lines set the mood for the poem and show it as the account of a spiritual quest in which the world is renounced, together with its false appearances, and the traditional upward path towards virtue and spiritual reality chosen. The ascent, its falls and difficulties, the contrasts between reality and appearances, continues until a summit is reached at stanza 4, when a new direction is then taken. There, at the peak, strange voices lead the journey from the world into another world where the poet no longer struggles but is 'led' by some unexplained spiritual power. In terms of mystical theology this new journey marks a possible transition from the meditative stage to the contemplative 'dark cloud of unknowing' described by St John of the Cross (1542–91) in his poem *En Una Noche Oscura*. The element of spiritual allegory in Vaughan's poem may be seen by referring to St John of the Cross's comments upon one of his own poems which is based on Solomon 4:17 (the source for the epigraph which Vaughan appends to 'Regeneration': 'Arise O North, and come thou South-wind, and blow upon my garden, that the spices thereof may flow out'). St John of the Cross interprets this biblical passage as a symbolic expression of the details of the spiritual life and the hidden relationship between God and the soul.

> By this breeze the soul here denotes the Holy Spirit, Who, as she says, awakens love; for, when this Divine breeze assails the soul, it enkindles it wholly and refreshes it and revives it and awakens the will and upraises the desires which aforetime had fallen and were asleep, to the love of God, in such manner that it may well be said thereof that it awakens the love both of the Spouse and of the Bride.*

This mystical interpretation helps to illustrate the background to Vaughan's poem, and also helps to explain its intensely symbolic language. The poet's visionary state leads him to an enclosed grove which is described in glowing archetypal and biblical terms which contrast strongly with the illusory appearance of the 'primros'd way' in the opening stanza. Here there is spring in winter, there are fragrances and a general sense of divine abundance, while the sun, as if it were a great alchemist's refining fire, shines equally upon all souls—'flowers'—and transforms them, whether they are awake or asleep, and a Pentecostal wind breathes over them at the direction of the divine will. As in Crashaw's 'Teresa' poems (but without their sensuousness) the climax is a prayer for mystical death.

---

* St John of the Cross, Spiritual Canticle, xxvi.3. Quoted in E: Allison Peers (ed.), *Complete Works of St John of the Cross*, Newman, Westminster, Vol.II, p.128.

'Vanity of Spirit'

'Vanity of Spirit' is again typical of the tenor of Part I with its emphasis on the yearning for spiritual knowledge and the difficulty of the quest. On this occasion the search is conducted through an examination of the Book of Nature rather than the scriptures; and it is remarkable for its rational and scientific approach. Here the scientific allusions of Donne or Herbert are used with far greater seriousness, and perhaps reflect the advances made by the natural sciences in the period. In a reference which recalls 'The World', Vaughan strives to comprehend 'Who bent the spheres, and circled in/ Corruption with this glorious ring'. He finds, however, that nature provides no clear answers; so he turns, instead, to study himself as if responding to the philosopher's precept 'know thyself' and anticipating Pope's line 'The proper study of mankind is Man'. Vaughan finds within his finite nature signs, 'weake beames and fires', which point towards his unique status and divine origins. This passage is a clear indication of how far Vaughan's theological position is removed from a strict Calvinistic insistence upon the absoluteness of the Fall, for these fragmented indications of his origins remind him that, however fallen, he is still a creature made in the image of God and that the image, while defaced, is not destroyed. But his efforts to reassemble the pieces and recreate the divine image within himself, and his effort to move beyond the 'glorious ring' which circles in the corruption of the finite world, both fail. Instead the poet is forced to accept that such endeavours are nothing but vanity, and that his reunion with the divine must lie beyond the grave.

'The Search'

'The Search' is similar to 'Vanity of Spirit' in that it too registers the limits of the intellect and of any attempt to achieve spiritual illumination through meditative and intellectual powers. Both are poems which by their use of the *via negativa* point out the failure of non-mystical means as vehicles to direct the soul toward God—and, consequently, of the need for the mystical. Both poems end in a blind alley of failure and darkness, but a darkness which—if accepted—is also the prelude to divine grace.

'The Search' begins as if it were a meditation; its context, the poet's night-long vigil of prayer and meditation upon God—a 'roving Extasie/ To find my Saviour'. In short, as an introduction to meditation, the poet's imagination has been dwelling upon the Bible and exerting itself in various compositions of place which range through both the Old

Testament and New Testament landscapes. The dramatic interest of the account is that the poet is always too late: the human resources of meditation—whether mind, memory, or imagination—fail to bring him to the end of his search. Even when he meditates upon the Passion of Christ, he only reaches through to *'Idæa's* of his Agonie'—when he desires Christ himself. As in 'Regeneration', the movement is arrested by a voice speaking from without the poem—'I heard one singing thus' —and the form of the poem switches from speech-couplets to lyrical song. The direction is to 'Search well another world; who studies this, / Travels in clouds, seeks *Manna*, where none is.' Again the poem moves towards the limits of the natural world and shows that essential reality belongs to another dimension of experience altogether.

'Ascension-day' and 'Ascension-Hymn'

This pair of poems opens the second part of *Silex Scintillans*. Both elegantly demonstrate the shift of emphasis from nostalgia for the lost innocence and perfection of Eden (which Vaughan particularly associates with childhood), to a vision of God's purpose at the end of time. Christ's Ascension provides 'Ascension-day' with the basic Christian model of human participation by spiritual ascent into another world: 'I soar and rise/ Up to the skies,/ Leaving the world their day.' While the poems show Vaughan's use of meditative techniques associated with St Ignatius, especially in his vivid 'composition of place' (the imaginative construction of a scene), the tone of joyful expectation is characteristic. The outburst of song suggests the dynamic energy of the poet's visionary imagination bursting the confines of the meditative exercise and its intellectual restraints.

By contrast, 'Ascension-Hymn' is a vivid description, by means of traditional images, of spiritual ascension: it shows the movement from flesh to spirit, earth to heaven, darkness to light; and, in the manner of any successful hymn, displays an unforced synthesis of various traditional images and references. This is most obvious in the succeeding cluster of images. These are both biblically based, and look expectantly towards the end of the world: the description of the refiner's fire and fuller's soap comes from the prophet Malachi (3:2), while the future in which God will 'Bring bone to bone/ And rebuild man' recalls the vision of the prophet Ezekiel in the valley of dry bones (Ezekiel 37). No poem so clearly places the poet's anguish at the lost perfection of Eden within his vision of the final purpose of God:

> Man of old
> Within the line
> Of *Eden* could

Like the Sun shine
All naked, innocent and bright,
And intimate with Heav'n, as light;

But since he
That brightness soil'd,
His garments be
All dark and spoil'd,
And here are left as nothing worth,
Till the Refiners fire breaks forth.

'They are all gone into the world of light!'

This untitled meditation upon death virtually counterpoints 'The World' in Part I, except that here the tension is derived from the poet's frustration with the material of finite being itself—though it allows 'some strange thoughts transcend our wonted theams,/ And into glory peep.' There remains a longing for transcendence; and, in this context, the image of the bird (the ancient symbol for the human soul in its cage of flesh) is appropriate and evocative. Here death itself becomes a beauty and treasure which releases the spirit into the glory of eternity:

I see them walking in an Air of glory,
    Whose light doth trample on my days:
My days, which are at best but dull and hoary,
    Meer glimmering and decays.

This poem belongs to a substantial tradition, and many features within it can be related to other poets. For example, the glowing opening line is one of the trademarks of the Metaphysical school that Vaughan shares. Indeed, the thought is not original: as with so many of Vaughan's poems, ideas (and versification), it can be found in Herbert—for instance, in his 'Pilgrimage' where Herbert remarks 'After so foul a journey death is fair,/ And but a chair.' However, Vaughan's originality lies in his capacity to suggest the quality of a spiritual experience, of vision and the sense of transcendence itself.

'The Night'

'The Night' is probably the occasion when Vaughan comes closest to achieving what may be considered a mystical poem. This is particularly true of the second part of the poem where the lines recall the poems of St John of the Cross. Vaughan begins with a biblical basis, the story of Nicodemus (John 3:2), which he refers to by an epigraph, but which is further enriched by a haunting mystical undertone, for example in the various images of light. This biblical basis allows the poet to establish the conceit or religious paradox upon which the poem is based: that night, not day, is the means of approach to God; and to develop a witty series of qualities through which night and darkness are described (lines 25–30).

At line 31 a new movement begins within the poem which draws upon the tradition of the Song of Solomon and which approaches most closely the poetry of St John of the Cross: the figures of the Beloved and Lover are traditionally used to describe the soul waiting for the coming of the Lord. The movement of the poem has thus shifted from the meditative style with its historical references and its composition of place, to a realm where God is the active power, and where the soul passively keeps a 'dumb watch' and awaits 'His knocking time'. The subsequent stanzas relate something of the nature of the mystic's 'dark night of the soul'. The experience evades description, and Vaughan is conscious of his distance from the reality which has briefly visited him; as it recedes he voices his discontent with the world about him and his place in it, and remains to hunger again for a sense of that spiritual absolute. The oxymoron in the final stanza, 'dazzling darkness', draws upon the paradoxical nature of a mystical tradition where God can only be 'seen' by 'darkness'; it also shows the sheer difficulty of finding language to express religious experience and, perhaps, the limits of poetry itself:

> There is in God (some say)
> A deep, but dazzling darkness; As men here
> Say it is late and dusky, because they
>   See not all clear;
>   O for that night! where I in him
>   Might live invisible and dim.

'L'Envoy'

This, the last of the poems, completes the thrust of the mystic vision, which reaches beyond the world. Here the speaker assumes the pose of one near death who bids farewell and looks eagerly forward to the perfection and transformation of all things.

>   Arise, arise!
> And like old cloaths fold up these skies,
> This long worn veyl: then shine and spread
> Thy own bright self over each head,
> And through thy creatures pierce and pass
> Till all becomes thy cloudless glass,
> Transparent as the purest day.

Not many poets have so clearly valued the natural world, felt its beauty to be touched by something divine, and yet felt its insufficiency and the need for its transformation. Even more rare are poets who have both, on the one hand, so powerfully expressed the quality of visionary experience and made it momentarily accessible, and on the other— while still using simple, natural diction and imagery—suggested a sense of light, transparency and spirit.

Chapter 8

Thomas Traherne

Introduction

> When I came into the Country, and being seated among silent Trees, had all my Time in mine own Hands, I resolved to Spend it all, whatever it cost me, in Search of Happiness, and to Satiat that burning Thirst which Nature had Enkindled in me from my Youth. In which I was so resolut, that I chose rather to live upon 10 pounds a yeer, and to go in Lether Clothes, and feed upon Bread and Water, so that I might hav all my time clearly to my self: then to keep many thousands per Annums in an Estate of Life where my Time would be Devoured in Care and Labor. (*Centuries*, III.46)*

The remarkable style and thought of these few lines of prose from Traherne's *Centuries*, the sense of vision and a unity of purpose which underwrites them, helps to illustrate where he stands in regard to the other Metaphysical and devotional poets amongst whom he is ranked. With them he shares a number of features which can be briefly summarised: the best religious verse of the period was written by amateur poets influenced by the example of Donne; all were strongly influenced by the temper and customs of the Anglican Church, and by those social and political tensions which culminated in the turmoil of the Civil War. To Donne's seminal influence, each of these poets added discoveries of his own. So to Donne's dramatic, colloquial and logical structures Herbert added lyrical innovation, Crashaw emotional ingenuity, and Vaughan an emphasis that was more personal and closer to the mystical. In this tradition Thomas Traherne (1637–74) marks both continuations and departures. He looks back to the Metaphysicals: there are echoes of Vaughan, Herbert and the influence of Donne in his work, though the style is quite different. But he is unique in his energy and the way in which his consciousness is so individual; indeed his range of address is sometimes so private that it almost anticipates aspects of Romanticism. In his subject matter, even more than Vaughan, he stands apart: secular, political or amorous themes are

---

* Quoted in Anne Ridler (ed.), *Thomas Traherne: Poems, Centuries and Three Thanksgivings*, Oxford University Press, London, 1966. Unless otherwise indicated, all quotations from Traherne's works are from this edition.

entirely absent from his works; instead he is unflinchingly, sometimes bafflingly, otherworldly.

Traherne's story is one of the exciting discoveries of modern scholarship. During his lifetime only one work was published, the anti-Catholic polemical *Roman Forgeries*. Soon after his death the excessively discursive *Christian Ethicks* (1675) appeared, followed in 1699 by the *Thanksgivings*. The major works, however, the *Centuries of Meditations* and the poems, were not published until a folio was discovered in a London bookstall in the late nineteenth century and subsequently identified and published by Bertram Dobell (1842–1914) in 1903. One other copy of Traherne's poems is held by the British Museum; called *Poems of Felicity* it was edited by Philip Traherne, Thomas's brother, who made some ill-advised textual changes. The result is that Traherne's texts are in some cases suspect and that our understanding is liable to be amended as further manuscripts are discovered—such as has occurred with the discovery of Traherne's *Select Meditations*.*

Life

Of simple origins—he was the son of a shoemaker in Hereford—Traherne was blessed with a kindly and prosperous relative, Philip Traherne, an inn-keeper and twice mayor of Hereford, who enabled him to be educated at Brasenose College, Oxford, where he took his BA in 1656. Nothing is known of Traherne's life from then until the Restoration but after the Restoration he was ordained by the Bishop of Oxford, given his MA and in 1661 presented to the parish of Credenhill in Herefordshire which he retained until his death (although someone else must have acted as minister to Credenhill when Traherne later moved to London). The influence of the years at Credenhill may underlie the intense visionary apprehension of nature which is a distinctive feature of his work.

A man of scholarly interests, his studies continued at Oxford during the time at Credenhill, and he received his BD degree in 1669. From about 1667 he also held a post in London as Chaplain to the Keeper of the Great Seal, Sir Orlando Bridgeman, and in addition, he was Vicar of Teddington in Middlesex, where he was buried on 10 October 1674. The years in London were full of literary activity: during this time the main prose works were completed and prepared for publication. The major prose work for which he is valued, the *Centuries*, is a series of spiritual directions which, it is believed, were written either for the wealthy and pious Susanna Hopton (née Harvey) of Kingston, some fifteen miles from Credenhill, for whom Traherne was a spiritual adviser;

* James M. Osborn, 'A New Traherne MS', *Times Literary Supplement*, 8 October 1964.

or else—and this is somewhat less likely—for a religious circle led by her. It is not clear whether these meditations were all written during Traherne's time in London, or begun while he was still in Credenhill, though it seems likely that had these meditations and directions been composed at Credenhill they would never have been written into the manuscript notebook form in which they were later discovered by Dobell. Susanna Hopton also played a more direct role in Traherne's work. She arranged for the publication of his *Thanksgivings* in 1699, and she may herself have written the preface to the first edition with its complimentary description of the author:

> He was a man of a cheerful and sprightly Temper, free from any thing of the sourness or formality, by which some great pretenders of Piety rather disparage and misrepresent true Religion, than recommend it; and therefore was very affable and pleasant in his Conversation, ready to do all good Offices to his Friends, and Charitable to the Poor almost beyond his ability.*

Style

In many respects the style of Traherne's prose is the same as that of his poetry: it is moulded and characterised by a type of 'enthusiasm' typical of the Interregnum (the period during which England was without a monarch and under the control of Cromwell and his followers). In some respects, Traherne deceives us by appearances. For instance, 'The Author to the Critical Peruser' opens the collection of his poems with a bold declaration about his style. In the manner of a follower of the Royal Society the poet proclaims an interest in 'The naked Truth' and rejects the flights of 'idle Fancies, Toys and Words'.

> No curling Metaphors that gild the Sence,
> Nor Pictures here, nor painted Eloquence;
> No florid Streams of Superficial Gems,
> But real Crowns and Thrones and Diadems!
> That Gold on Gold should hiding shining ly
> May well be reckon'd baser Heraldry.

Yet Traherne is no rationalist, and he achieves a more mystical kind of eloquence. For example, the style of the *Thanksgivings* draws copiously upon the Psalms, and is marked by rhythms that are closer to those of poetry than of prose. His prose is elevated as if inspired, and thoughts flow and merge into one another by rapid association. In fact, association seems to be the ordering principle of his writing, rather

---

* Quoted in Anne Ridler (ed.), *Thomas Traherne: Poems, Centuries and Three Thanksgivings*, p.xii.

than logical progression from one thought to another. Abstract nouns and adjectives abound; nouns and exclamations accumulate, held together loosely by conjunctions. Some sentences have no verbs. The effect is chaotic, repetitious and inspirational—as if the writer were striving for something beyond the limits of syntax and logical thought.

The style of Traherne's verse is as distinctive as his prose and stands in contrast to that of the other Metaphysicals. As were nearly all poets of the time he was influenced by Donne, but the precise nature of that influence on his own style is difficult to pinpoint: certainly it does not appear upon the surface of the poems; for example, unlike Donne, he does not employ any 'Metaphysical' conceits. But in both prose and poetry he shows a remarkable unity of vision which helps account for the degree to which he repeats the same essential ideas throughout his works. In contrast to Herbert, whose 'To All Angels and Saints' he copied into one of his manuscript books, he lacks that acute, delicate sense of metre, form and balance that is such a feature of Herbert's work. In contrast to Crashaw, the extraordinary limits of expression, the element of the grotesque which arrests attention, are alien to Traherne. Vaughan, to whom he is generally closest in thought, and to whom the eminent literary scholar Alexander Grosart (1827–99) first assigned Traherne's poems when they were discovered, has a common touch which Traherne lacks. Where Vaughan remains closer to the world of ordinary experience, and his expression slow, often laboured and emotionally restrained, Traherne is ecstatic, his vision so mystical, his sensibility so unrestrained by a normal grasp of the world, that he leaves the average reader perplexed.

His style is direct and simple. Its dominant characteristic is a sheer exuberant vitality of vision: an unfettered delight in the world; an appreciation of God's goodness and of the whole of creation. Exclamations and direct address to God are commonplace, and the heroic couplet is the dominant form. The use of capital letters should be noted; they indicate points of emphasis of expression—as in music. To command attention to invariably religious subjects, he depends upon vigour of expression: he does not provide surprise or lyrical delights.

Thought

Traherne's distinctive style is the appropriate medium for his thought. In the meditative and mystical tradition of the Church he is an exponent of the 'affirmative way'—an aspect of mystical theology that teaches the believer to make his approach to God through positive assertions about the divine nature, for instance its goodness and power. (The converse of the affirmative way is the *via negativa* which approaches God through negation, by denying that any words may describe him, or any predicates be attached to him.) Fittingly for a poet who appears to have been naturally inclined to speak positively about the divine nature and its goodness, Traherne exhibits a spirituality which makes considerable use of feelings and emotions. In the *Centuries* he shows a way of regarding the world which indicates that the *via negativa*, with its affirmation of divine transcendence by a denial of likeness between the finite and the infinite, would have been uncongenial to him: he remarks that 'Great Offence hath been don by the Philosophers and Scandal given, through their Blindness, many of them in making Felicity to consist in Negativs . . . For it is the Affront of Nature, a making vain the Powers, and a Baffling the Expectations of the Soul, to deny it all Objects, and a Confining it to the Grave, and a Condemning of it to Death to tie it to that inward unnatural mistaken Self sufficiency and Contentment they talk of' (C.II.100).*

This leads naturally to a consideration of Traherne's theological outlook and also his much-criticised religious optimism. His theology is based upon a method which is heavily dependent upon the insights of mystical experience—insights gained through the contemplation of nature. Where appropriate, however, he supports his views with instances from historical religion, and he consistently places a very high estimate upon human reason and its role in the stages of mystical progression. What is worth noticing, however, is that Traherne appears to give human reason a rather special and comprehensive meaning, since he expands it to imply something like the total personality. He bases his understanding of man upon the theological idea of the *imago dei*, which teaches that man is made 'in the image of God' and that, possessing this image as an innate spiritual faculty, he is naturally inclined to seek God. The effect of this belief on Traherne's writing is reminiscent of St Augustine in his *Confessions*, since he uses both human needs and desires as pointers towards God, and then, by frequent repetitions, attempts to clarify or in some way reveal his essential self.

In the absolute sense of Renaissance Neoplatonism Traherne is concerned with divine wisdom, but he does not sacrifice scripture to Platonism. From the commonplace range of sources—the Hermetic writers, Platonists and theologians—he gleans materials which he then refashions in a striking and individual way. He quotes frequently from the Florentine Academy, Pico della Mirandola and Hermes Trismegistus, and has been compared to Cambridge Platonists such as John Smith (1618–52); no other 'Metaphysical' so deliberately follows a philosophy and expounds it. One scholar's description of this aspect of

* References to the *Centuries* will include the Century and Meditation number as used above.

Neoplatonism is appropriate for Traherne, for whom 'The highest human wisdom is a blinding intellectual vision of Wisdom and a mystical union with It. Caught up by God and formed by Him, the Intellect which contemplates divine things is then renewed and transformed into the same shape with God and becomes one spirit with Him.'*

With the vision of God as his aim, Traherne's method is free of the Calvinistic pessimism about human nature which pervades so much seventeenth-century theology, and which Vaughan's work occasionally illustrates. Many readers have been impressed by the curious absence of a sense of evil in Traherne's work, and some have regarded this as a sign of his naivety. They are mistaken. His apparent omission of evil is neither incidental nor naive: his emphasis is upon regaining spiritual vision rather than lamenting Original Sin. No other writer so vividly recreates a sense of primal, Edenic innocence. The image he most commonly identifies with is that of the new-born child who symbolises both the unfallen state and his own consciousness. Traherne's individual concern is vital here, he wishes to teach individuals how they may attain fulfilment; and once it is accepted that this individual quest is his dominant concern, his much discussed 'doctrine of pleasure or enjoyment' is more readily understood. The concept is strongly influenced by the general nature of Neoplatonist thought, in particular its notion that the soul is 'imprisoned' in the body. Bearing in mind that for Traherne soul and mind appear to be the same thing, it becomes apparent that he takes the Neoplatonist relationship of the soul to the body to be an image of the Fall of Adam and Eve from their original spiritual perfection in Eden, and that he believes that each individual soul must seek reunion with divine reality which is—by definition—spiritual and perfect. The innovative aspect of the concept, however, appears in Traherne's opinion that this divine perfection was *already* present within the world, and that the mind/soul could experience reunion with God through a proper understanding or 'enjoyment' of the world. This proper, soul-transforming enjoyment of the world is achieved through mystical contemplation in which the soul is moulded by the nature of that which it 'contemplates', for as Traherne observes, 'The Contemplation of Eternity maketh the Soul Immortal' (C.I.55).

At this point the contrast of Traherne with Vaughan and the other Metaphysicals is most marked. Unlike Vaughan, whom he most closely resembles among the Metaphysicals, Traherne offers, on the one hand, little or no insight into the mystical experience of the dark night of the soul, while, on the other hand, his appreciation of nature is even keener. Vaughan's spirituality is ultimately world-renouncing; for him

---

* Eugene Rice, *The Renaissance Idea of Wisdom*, Harvard University Press, Cambridge, Massachusetts, 1958, p.67.

natural beauty, however much an occasion of joy and illumination, merely sharpens the sense of the loss of the original perfection of Eden, and is accompanied by grief. In sharp contrast to this, for Traherne the flight from the physical to the spiritual does not occur. Instead he consciously 'spiritualises' the temporal and discerns within it the means of glory: 'Never was any thing in this World loved too much' (C.II.66). However, he is careful to make clear the distinction between a proper and an improper use of the world, for instance in the same passage he remarks how 'many Things have been loved in a fals Way.' In this sense his poems and meditations provide a remarkable account of how to contemplate the divine through the world in a 'true' way.

Prose works

In common with many of the other Metaphysical and mystical writers during the Interregnum, Traherne's work is characterised by a diffuse, vague quality. His major theological and ethical works, all published anonymously, embody a personal vision that addresses spiritual concerns rather than social or moral codes. And in these prose works the sense of a shaping spirit relates them to the poems. Even his *Roman Forgeries* (1673), which has been described as bearing the marks of a thesis for the BD, is marked by a liveliness of spirit on what is now a dull—though then controversial—subject. *Christian Ethicks* is a masterly blend of scholarly reflection and practical wisdom in an elegant and spirited style upon such topics as courage, charity and generosity of spirit. The relation to the poems can be seen both in the way poems were included in the text, and in the content and style of the prose itself. For example, this passage from the chapter 'Of Knowledge':

> The sphere of its activity [the Soul] is illimited, its energy is endless upon all its objects. It can exceed the heavens in its operations, and run out into infinite spaces. Such is the extent of knowledge that it seemeth to be the Light of all Eternity. All objects are equally near to the splendour of its beams: As innumerable millions may be conceived in its Light, with a ready capacity for millions more; so can it penetrate all abysses, reach to the centre of all Nature, converse with all beings, visible and invisible, corporeal and spiritual, temporal and eternal, created and increated, finite and infinite, substantial and accidental, actual and possible, imaginary and real; all the mysteries of bliss and misery, all the secrets of heaven and hell are objects of the Soul's capacity, and shall be actually seen and known here.*

* Quoted by Dobell in his Introduction to his edition of Traherne's poems (1903) and included in G.I. Wade (ed.), *The Poetical Works of Thomas Traherne*, Cooper Square, New York, 1965, pp. LXIVL—XV.

This is a cogent demonstration of his thought in practice, in particular his sense of vision, both intellectual and mystical, which is reached through a proper appreciation of the cosmos.

It is in the *Centuries* that Traherne's visionary prose and thought reaches its most eloquent expression in a style which approximates that of poetry. Here again the work is interspersed with poems. It is formally divided into a series of reflections in numbered paragraphs upon various religious subjects and with some autobiographical allusions. There are four complete *Centuries*, while the fifth has only ten paragraphs. The work is prefaced with a brief verse dedication, considered to be to Susanna Hopton:

This book unto the friend of my best friend
As of the Wisest Love a Mark I send
That she may write my Makers prais therin
And make her self therby a Cherubin.

The unique mystical vision which looms in every paragraph can be gauged by the following:

You never Enjoy the World aright, till the Sea itself floweth in your Veins, till you are Clothed with the Heavens, and Crowned with the Stars ... (C.I.29).

Some of the passages anticipate William Blake (1757–1827)—such as Traherne's remark 'Infinit Wants Satisfied Produce infinit Joys' (C.I.43)—while others, particularly the autobiographical sections where he dwells on the visions of childhood, are reminiscent of early Wordsworth, particularly the 'Intimations' ode. In the 'Third Century' Traherne provides some of his most memorable expressions of a brilliant and glowing vision of the world from early childhood:

The Corn was Orient and Immortal Wheat, which never should be reaped, nor was ever sown. I thought it had stood from Everlasting to Everlasting. The Dust and Stones of the Street were as Precious as GOLD. The Gates were at first the End of the World, The Green Trees when I saw them first through one of the Gates Transported and Ravished me; their Sweetness and unusual Beauty made my Heart to leap, and almost mad with Extasie, they were such strange and Wonderfull Thing[s]: The Men! O what Venerable and Reverend Creatures did the Aged seem! Immortal Cherubims! And yong Men Glittering and Sparkling Angels and Maids strange Seraphick Pieces of Life and Beauty! Boys and Girls Tumbling in the Street, and Playing, were moving Jewels. I knew not that they were Born or should Die. But all things abided Eternaly as they were in their Proper Places. Eternity was Manifest in the Light of the Day, and

som thing infinit Behind evry thing appeared: which talked with my
Expectation and moved my Desire. The Citie seemed to stand in
Eden, or to be Built in Heaven . . . (C.III.3).

Poems

Although the ordering of Traherne's poems is largely conjectural, the
evenness of his style is remarkable—very few poems being clearly less
successful than the others—and the reading of his poetry is enhanced
when the poems are read together. This effect is mainly due to two
reasons: first, because the poems tell something of Traherne's spiritual
journey, and second, because they also proceed from his unity of
vision. This unity of vision raises the common accusation that Traherne's poetry is limited because of its repetitiveness. It is true that certain themes or motifs consistently reappear: for example, the spiritual-
isation of the material world ('Wonder'); childhood as the paradigm
for a time of vision which must be regained ('Innocence'); the need to
perceive or 'love' the world correctly ('The Preparative'); the necessity
to use the world and the unity between flesh and spirit ('My Spirit',
'The Estate'). But within the constraints of a limited perspective he is
masterful. Indeed, the consistency of his religious subject, and his
essential approach to it, means that the individual accomplishment of
each poem is enhanced when read alongside the others. Such a reading
allows the reader to appreciate Traherne's capacity to interweave his
subject, as a musician does in his variations upon a central theme, with
variations of understanding, variety of expression, and vitality.

'Wonder'

The first five stanzas of this eight-stanza poem indicate something of
Traherne's achievement as a poet, his characteristic style and the links
between his thought, prose and poetry. As with many of his poems, it
recalls his prose: in this case the fifth stanza echoes Century III.2,3
(part of which is quoted above, p.139). The essence of the style is its
undiluted vitality, its vivid expression of delight and its powerful evo-
cation of a state of heightened spiritual consciousness.

The sense of structure within the poem demonstrates Traherne's
craftsmanship. A range of techniques for conveying ecstasy dominate;
these include the frequent use of direct address, exclamations, capitals
and typographical variations. Characteristically, each stanza varies its
line lengths to suggest the development of thought and to permit its
emphasis—as indeed can also be seen in Herbert and Vaughan—with
the maximum emphasis being delayed until the final and shortest line.

In thought and sense the poem is essentially simple. Traherne deals with the state of primal innocence and wonder which is the basis for contemplation, and of which childhood is his model, as indeed it is in scripture (Mark 10:14–15). The exuberance of these stanzas, and their unqualified wonder at the sheer beauty of the world, are unrivalled:

> How like an Angel came I down!
> How Bright are all Things here!
> When first among his Works I did appear
> O how their GLORY me did Crown?
> The World resembled his *Eternitie*,
> In which my Soul did Walk;
> And evry Thing that I did see,
> Did with me talk.

The simile which expresses this simple thought in the opening line recalls Vaughan's 'Angel-infancy' in 'Retreat', but beyond this coincidence the poems and ideas are distinct. Vaughan's poem is dominated by the tone of regret and nostalgia, the longing to be free of the world; in direct contrast to this, Traherne immerses himself in the world and exults in a transforming unalloyed vision. Behind this are, of course, the religious symbols of the First Garden and the First Man, Eden and Adam. Traherne does not deny the Fall of mankind from original perfection, but he ignores it. His concern is with the fact of spiritual experience, and the imagery which recalls Eden's perfection is the most natural instrument through which he can express that experience of communion with God and the perception of the spiritual in and through the creation.

> The Skies in their Magnificence,
> The Lively, Lovely Air;
> Oh how Divine, how soft, how Sweet, how fair!
> The stars did entertain my Sence,
> And all the Works of GOD so Bright and pure,
> So Rich and Great did seem,
> As if they ever must endure,
> In my Esteem.
>
> A Native Health and Innocence
> Within my Bones did grow,
> And while my GOD did all his Glories shew,
> I felt a Vigour in my Sence
> That was all SPIRIT. I within did flow
> With Seas of Life, like Wine;
> I nothing in the World did know,
> But 'twas Divine.
>
> Harsh ragged Objects were conceald,
> Oppressions Tears and Cries,

Sins, Griefs, Complaints, Dissentions, Weeping Eys,
  Were hid: and only Things reveald,
Which Heav'nly Spirits, and the Angels prize.
    The State of Innocence
  And Bliss, not Trades and Poverties,
    Did fill My Sence.

The Streets were pavd with Golden Stones,
  The Boys and Girles were mine,
Oh how did all their Lovly faces shine!
  The Sons of Men were Holy Ones.
Joy, Beauty, Welfare did appear to me,
  And evry Thing which here I found,
  While like an Angel I did see,
    Adornd the Ground. (stanzas 2–5)

The movement of the poem through these stanzas suggests the transformation of the physical world as experienced in a state of contemplation. As stanza 4 shows, the poet does not deny the existence of evil, but he denies its power over his soul. In this sense his visionary perception of the world reverses the Fall. In the succeeding stanzas, particularly 7 and 8, he shows that he does not restrict his vision to nature but extends it to all the things of the world. Even the most material of human desires, possessions, can be contemplated in this way:

Proprieties themselves were mine,
  And Hedges Ornaments;
Walls, Boxes, Coffers, and their rich Contents
  Did not Divide my Joys, but shine.
Clothes, Ribbans, Jewels, Laces, I esteemd
  My Joys by others worn;
  For me they all to wear them seemd
    When I was born. (stanza 8)

The state of awareness towards which the poem presses is that of felicity. Traherne's closure in the final line, which turns back to the memory of childhood in the first stanza, gives the poem a sense of emotional fullness and completeness. But there is no sense that this implies the poet is locked in by his past, and that this cannot be achieved in the life of the adult. The child is the paradigm, just as Eden and Adam are the biblical and symbolic models. Traherne's capacity to transform finite experience, his glowing assertion of the freedom of the spirit to enjoy all things rather than be confined by notions of possession, remains probably the most impressive statement of its kind within English literature, and, within the company of devotional poets, gives him an honoured place.

Chapter 9

Andrew Marvell

Introduction

Among the Metaphysical poets few can offer so sharp a contrast to the developments initiated by Donne and his successors than Andrew Marvell (1621–78). Whereas Herbert, Crashaw, Vaughan and Traherne tend to press towards a spiritual vision, and gradually confine their poetry, both in style and subject, to what will express that dimension of experience, Marvell is wholly immersed in the political and social pressures of the period, and, both in their style and content, his prose and poetry reflect the extent and consequences of that involvement. Indeed, it was not until this century, under the influence of such critics as Sir Herbert Grierson and T.S. Eliot, that Marvell was appreciated as a poet and not merely a Commonwealth and Restoration political writer and satirist.

Today, his reputation as a poet assured, Marvell remains an enigmatic figure—a chameleon poet. Consistently sensitive and responsive to his milieu, he nevertheless succeeded in preserving an unusual degree of objectivity. Ironical and perceptive in his portrayal of ideas and tensions, he generally withheld any statement of his personal position on any matter—unless as a matter of policy. During the Civil War he appears to have moved between Royalist and Parliamentary sides with some agility. He transferred support from Charles to Cromwell, and then from Cromwell to Parliament, and then finally back to the Royalist cause and Charles II during the Restoration. It would, however, be unfair to regard him as treacherous. Shifts in allegiance were common during the troubled circumstances of the time, and they reflect the profound uncertainty of many patriotic Englishmen as to exactly what was the right course of action in a situation of national crisis where no cause appeared irreproachable. This dilemma of allegiance is reflected in Marvell's poetry, most particularly in the way his views of Charles I and Cromwell appear equivocal because of their subtle ironies of tone and allusion.

It is difficult to place the style of Marvell's poetry in any one tradition. At times his sympathies seem those of a Cavalier poet: yet on other occasions he appears more closely aligned with the Puritan faction. In literature, he draws upon Jonson and the Spenserians nearly as much as upon the Metaphysicals. In other words, he utilises the literary traditions available to him and recreates them to his own various purposes so that, for example, a genre such as the pastoral is endowed with a wholly new depth and subtlety of meaning. His versatility is so great that the quest for a shaping spirit in his work seems futile: equally able to compose an intense devotional lyric in the manner of Herbert, or to handle an extended conceit in the manner of Donne, no one style is uniquely his own.

Life

Since most of Marvell's lyric poetry was written in a comparatively short period between the 1640s and early 1650s, it is not enough to depend upon his poetry to illustrate either the essential aspects of his life, or the relationship between his life and his writing in its various forms. Nevertheless, scholars, such as H.M. Margoliouth, Pierre Legouis and John Dixon Hunt, have attempted to provide the various poems with historical and biographical circumstances, and their efforts do suggest a connection between his life and works which is more intimate than is claimed for any other poet in the Metaphysical tradition.

A Yorkshireman, Marvell was born at Winestead in Holderness on 31 March 1621. His father, an Anglican clergyman of liberal views, ensured his son's education at Hull Grammar School and then at Trinity College, Cambridge, at a time when the university was a microcosm of the religious conflicts which troubled England, and when great Platonist philosophers, such as John Smith and Benjamin Whichcote, both dominated its intellectual life and antagonised and revivified the Puritan spirit by their greater inclination towards toleration and mysticism. While at Peterhouse College, then a centre for Roman Catholic influences, Marvell may even have met Richard Crashaw. Indeed, one of the interesting rumours about Marvell during these years is the story that claims he was converted by Jesuit agents while he was still at Peterhouse, and that he fled to London before being found and returned to College by his father.

Most of Marvell's lyrics date from the 1640s to the 1650s. These years cover the period from when he left Cambridge, to when he was elected Member of Parliament for Hull (1659)—a seat he held until his death.

Marvell left Cambridge in 1641 and, appropriately for one trained as a Renaissance humanist, undertook a tour of the Continent—perhaps while holding the position of tutor to a wealthy gentleman's son. This involved him in a protracted absence from England, indeed the four years he travelled were the time when many of his friends and contemporaries in England were embroiled in the miseries of the Civil War. He visited Rome in 1645, as his lampoon on the English priest and poet Richard Flecknoe (*d.*?1678) records, and probably also the Netherlands, France and Spain. Although the influence of the Continent upon his poetry is a complicated subject, various images, lines and the general tenor of his thought can be fruitfully related to the famous European scenes, personalities and cultural influences he would have encountered.

Early in 1648 Marvell returned to England and wrote a number of poems which betray some trace of Royalist leanings, for instance, such poems as 'To His Noble Friend Mr Richard Lovelace'. Soon after Cromwell's return from Ireland (1650) Marvell wrote the 'Horatian Ode' with its more disengaged view of the complicated practical and ethical issues represented by the leadership of both Charles I and Cromwell. Events moved quickly during this period. Marvell returned to his native Yorkshire as tutor to the daughter of General Fairfax (1612–71) who had retired to Nun Appleton after resigning his post as General of the Army on 25 July 1650 as a protest against the invasion of Scotland. Nun Appleton became the inspiration for some of Marvell's most remarkable works in the tradition of country house and pastoral poetry, but at the same time the presence of Fairfax, the man of action who had sought retirement, stimulated Marvell to interweave his celebrations of the retired life with elements that recalled contemporary affairs and the world of action.

While Marvell's deep interest in the tension between the contemplative and active life figures in his Nun Appleton works, his move to London about 1653, and his employment as tutor at Eton to William Dutton— later to be Cromwell's ward—suggests his interest in playing a more active role in affairs. This interest is perhaps implicit in his undertaking the poem in honour of Cromwell, 'The First Anniversary of the Government under his Highness the Lord Protector' (1655). Marvell's aspiration to a public role was finally realised through the assistance of Milton, who was blind by this time, and Marvell was appointed to assist him as Latin Secretary to the Council of State (1657).

After his election to Parliament Marvell's view of Cromwell appears to have become less supportive. He became a forceful parliamentarian and was very dutiful in the service of his electorate, as can be seen in the numerous letters he wrote to his constituents at Hull. A major satirical prose work composed during the Restoration, *The Rehearsal Transpros'd* (1672), shows Marvell's continuing intelligent involvement in various crucial issues of the time. This period also saw, however, a slackening in his poetic activity.

Style

On the surface the trappings of the Metaphysical style are more
obvious in Marvell than in, say, Crashaw, Vaughan and Traherne.
Though the precise forms of his expression are unique, the dramatic
and metaphorical surface of the Metaphysical style is easily found in
Marvell's poetry where the various devices, such as conceits, emblems,
paradoxes, speculations, arguments, tensions and nuances of tone, are
common. Yet the need to consider him among the Metaphysical poets
is more than a matter of surface texture, and stems both from his
complex vision and his wit. Though often subtle and mocking, there is
in his poetry a consistent groundtone of anguished engagement with
life in which profoundly felt tensions, paradoxes and contradictions
are manipulated through irony and dialectic to achieve a complex
awareness.

Common to nearly all Marvell's poetry is a characteristic, multi-
faceted view which finds expression through ambiguity and irony, and
which, in a period fraught by factionalism and enthusiasm, suggests a
deliberate lack of commitment to any one point of view. Yet, although
unlike Donne or the devotional poets he claims no particular view of
life as his own, and apparently makes no attempt to achieve intellectual
coherence or spiritual renewal, for Marvell wit is still a means towards
essential truth, and poetry the most appropriate form for its
expression. Perhaps two of the most notable aspects of his poetry are
first, that its ironic and apparently detached manner is the instrument
through which he reflected upon the issues that perplexed his society,
and second, that we are impressed by his extraordinary ability to
express profound thought beneath such a deceptively lyrical, graceful
or witty surface.

A distinctive feature of Marvell's writing is his remarkable talent for
combining a variety of different literary styles and forms, rather than
favouring any one literary fashion or genre. He can blend both Metaphysical wit and Baroque complexity with Caroline grace. Similarly he
can write pastoral love lyrics which are reminiscent of the Spenserians,
while in the same poems exploring the deeper devotional and contemplative mode associated with Vaughan and Herbert.

A consistent feature of Marvell's writing is the way in which the
challenge of achieving a balance between contradictions seems particularly to fascinate him. Whatever order he achieves is only after some
struggle, and through the application of his practical common sense
and strength of mind. Whether it is the issues of free will and fate,
peace and war, the pleasures of a finite world and the longing for the
infinite, the consistent aim is to achieve a complicated balance or harmony of vision. Illustrations of this interest in balance are his various
explorations of the commonplace Renaissance debate over the relative

virtues of the contemplative and the active life. Milton considered this stock question in his pair of poems 'Il Penseroso' and 'L'Allegro', and it exercised Marvell's thoughts in a number of poems written during his time at Nun Appleton. Other instances of his interest in balance are his discrimination between the virtues of nature in its wild state, and nature as cultivated by man; and between the virtues of an executed but gracious king, and a calculating leader appropriate to the times.

The love poems frequently use the devices of the dialectical poetic debates of Caroline love poetry, but with greater substance and intellectual rigour than in the works of such poets as Cleveland, Suckling or Rochester (1648–80). For instance, in 'The Fair Singer' Marvell sets attitudes and qualities against one another, heart against mind, sight against sound, to surprise the reader by the relationship he establishes between them:

> To make a final conquest of all me,
> Love did compose so sweet an Enemy,
> In whom both Beauties to my death agree,
> Joyning themselves in fatal Harmony;
> That while she with her Eyes my Heart does bind,
> She with her Voice might captivate my Mind.*

Donne's witty treatment of love is echoed in 'The Definition of Love' where Marvell exploits some of Donne's images, as, for example, in his scientific allusions, and in such stylistic features as the delight in paradox and witty parenthesis. The poem explores what the poet regards as a fundamental tension between desire and fulfilment, and sets the actual condition of life against an ideal love:

> My Love is of a birth as rare
> As 'tis for object strange and high:
> It was begotten by despair
> Upon Impossibility.

In subsequent stanzas of the poem Marvell uses geometrical imagery to suggest the laws of nature or fate which confound a perfect love. With a nice swipe at hyperbole for such love, Marvell shows that idealistic love exists, constant always, precisely because it can never be fulfilled:

> As Lines so Loves *oblique* may well
> Themselves in every Angle greet:
> But ours so truly *Paralel*,
> Though infinite can never meet.

* Quoted in H.M. Margoliouth (ed.), *The Poems and Letters of Andrew Marvell*, Oxford University Press, Oxford, 3rd edition, 1971, Vol.1. All quotations from Marvell's works are from this edition.

The same interest in tensions can be found in his adaptations of the pastoral. For example, 'The Nymph complaining for the death of her Faun' provides, in addition to multiple meanings and massive implications, a sharp contrast between the states of pastoral illusion and human reality. Here pastoral innocence is violated by the world itself in the form of the troopers—a term consistently applied to the parliamentary army—who invade and destroy a cloistered and retired way of life. As its title suggests, the poem centres on the nymph who laments that the 'wanton Troopers' have shot her faun. The contrast between the beautifully elegant clean lines and the tough-minded conceit which concludes the poem, points towards the complex understanding of life which lurks beneath the accomplished surfaces of Marvell's poetry. In this world nothing may survive, not even compassion, unless it is 'cut in Marble':

> First my unhappy Statue shall
> But cut in Marble; and withal,
> Let it be weeping too: but there
> Th' Engraver sure his Art may spare;
> For I so truly thee bemoane,
> That I shall weep though I be Stone:
> Until my Tears, still dropping, wear
> My breast, themselves engraving there.

Prose

During his life as a parliamentarian Marvell engaged in few literary activities: such work as he produced was mainly prose, though he did write some verse satires which attacked corruption in Court, Parliament and Church. The most memorable of his prose works, *The Rehearsal Transpros'd* (1672), gave him the reputation, according to Bishop Gilbert Burnet (1643–1715), of being 'the liveliest droll of the age, who writ in a burlesque strain, but with so entertaining and peculiar a conduct, that from the king down to the tradesman his book was read with great pleasure.'*

The work takes its title from the play by the Duke of Buckingham (1628–87), *The Rehearsal* (performed 1671), and its satire is directed against the persecution of Nonconformists during the Restoration: in particular it criticises the intolerant attitudes expressed by such divines as the then Archdeacon of Canterbury, Samuel Parker (1640–88). In a flexible, exuberant style characterised by long paragraphs, parentheses and chatty asides, Marvell affirms humanitarianism and tolerance

* Quoted in Pierre Legouis, *Andrew Marvell: Poet, Puritan, Patriot*, Oxford University Press, Oxford, 1968, p.202.

against the oppressive intolerance of the Restoration Church. Bishop Burnet claimed that the style was burlesque but in point of fact Marvell anticipates some of the discoveries of such Augustan satiric masterpieces as Swift's *A Tale of a Tub* (1704) and Pope's *The Dunciad* (1728), his work showing that serious issues could be handled responsibly by the satirist's caricature.

The poems

Love lyrics

It is typical of Marvell that his poems defy the pigeon-holing of poetic types. For example, many of his poems that deploy the pastoral tradition deal with love in order to provoke a complex debate on the tensions between soul and body, innocence and experience, idealism and necessity. In those poems that are more directly recognisable as love lyrics, the same density of meaning underlies the lyric ease that Marvell drew from the Caroline poets.

In 'The Gallery' he uses the conceit of his soul as a gallery in which the diverse images of his mistress Clora form the pictures. The method is one of juxtaposition: she is variously depicted as an 'Inhumane Murtheresse', 'Aurora', 'Enchantress', 'Venus' and a 'Sheperdess'. While it is the last of these which he favours in a gracious compliment, it is the penultimate stanza upon which the poem turns and which demonstrates Marvell's talent for holding a series of possibilities together in one work to suggest the complexity of experience:

> These Pictures and a thousand more,
> Of Thee, my Gallery do store;
> In all the Forms thou can'st invent
> Either to please me, or torment:
> For thou alone to people me,
> Art grown a num'rous Colony;
> And a Collection choicer far
> Then or *White-hall's*, or *Mantua's* were.

'Mourning' is another love poem, this time in a more sceptical vein, which concentrates upon contraries and the reality of cause and effect. At its centre is a discussion of the meaning of Chlora's tears for her dead lover. Marvell places this discussion within a macrocosmic perspective: the 'Off-springs' he refers to pointing, on the one hand to Chlora's eyes as springs, and her tears as their infants, while, on the other hand, suggesting in a more universal way that human 'Off-spring' and Chlora's tears are subject to fate:

You, that decipher out the Fate
Of humane Off-springs from the Skies,
What mean these Infants which of late
Spring from the Starrs of *Chlora's* Eyes?

In the following stanzas the poet realises that Chlora's tears are not genuine but declines to accept any one explanation. The penultimate stanza is evasive and ambiguous: here Marvell expands the scope of the poem through the addition of dramatic physical action in the conceit of the pearl divers, and he plays on the word 'sound' (which in this context could be a verb meaning 'to plumb' or an adjective meaning '(un)reliable') to ensure that the final meaning is indecisive:

How wide they dream! The *Indian* Slaves
That sink for Pearl through Seas profound,
Would find her Tears yet deeper Waves
And not of one the bottom sound.

In the succeeding stanza, however, Marvell reverts to his uncommited stance where all possibilities are surveyed, and a more obvious innuendo and scepticism are expressed:

I yet my silent Judgement keep,
Disputing not what they believe:
But sure as oft as Women weep,
It is to be suppos'd they grieve.

Marvell's most famous poem, and the one most clearly in the tradition of the love poem, is 'To His Coy Mistress'. While on the surface of the poem he pursues the Renaissance theme of *carpe diem*, with its argument that you should enjoy yourself while you have the opportunity and its view that, given the brevity of life, a woman's coyness is folly, on a more profound level the poem deals with the paradoxical nature of time itself, in particular the fact that time is the agent of both decay and growth.

The opening direct address is a mock praise, or encomium, of a conventional coyness which would be appropriate 'Had we but World enough, and Time'. Marvell captures the bantering tone of the Cavalier adept in the stratagems of the love game, its reticences, ploys and verbal conventions. Yet Marvell is treacherous as a flatterer: his time span—'before the flood' and until 'the Conversion of the Jews'—encompasses all human history; his 'vegetable Love' is 'Vaster than Empires'. Such spatial monstrosities subvert, and finally dismiss, his pretence at admiration.

Moving from illusion to reality, from growth to decay, the second stanza marks an important shift in thought:

> But at my back I alwaies hear
> Times winged Charriot hurrying near:
> And yonder all before us lye
> Desarts of vast Eternity.
> Thy Beauty shall no more be found;
> Nor, in thy marble Vault, shall sound
> My ecchoing Song: then Worms shall try
> That long preserv'd Virginity:
> And your quaint Honour turn to dust;
> And into ashes all my Lust.
> The Grave's a fine and private place,
> But none I think do there embrace.

Here Marvell's forceful rhetoric introduces a Metaphysical shudder, a new grimness of thought and tone, which sharply contrasts with the preceding stanza. Infinite space has now become a sterile desert which finally contracts into the narrow compass of the grave. On the one hand, Marvell's argument at this point seems that of the libertine determined to seduce his mistress, but it is significant that lust too is reduced 'into ashes'. Here love is conquered by the reality of time.

The final stanza appears to relieve the grimness of this analysis by stressing the intensity of the moment, but even here passionate affirmations are undermined:

> Now therefore, while the youthful hew
> Sits on thy skin like morning dew,
> And while thy willing Soul transpires
> At every pore with instant Fires,
> Now let us sport us while we may;
> And now, like am'rous birds of prey,
> Rather at once our Time devour.
> Than languish in his slow-chapt pow'r.
> Let us roll all our Strength, and all
> Our sweetness, up into one Ball:
> And tear our Pleasures with rough strife,
> Thorough the Iron gates of Life.
> Thus, though we cannot make our Sun
> Stand still, yet will make him run.

This stanza has been read as a forceful argument for sexual pleasure—'let us sport us while we may'—and its quick movements suggest the passion of sexual consummation. Yet its tone and imagery imply far more. The lovers oppose time by 'devouring it'; by supposedly doing this the lovers themselves replace and reflect Time's 'winged Charriot' as they become 'am'rous birds of prey'. This is itself a subversive image.

It implies that their active devouring of Time won't really frustrate Time, but merely accelerate its processes of decay. Another more ironical view may be provided by recollection of the tradition of the Renaissance emblems concerning such images as 'Ball' and 'Iron': the interpretation of such emblems used the exploding cannon-ball as an image of that higher wisdom which was achieved only when man, in harmony with both his own powers and those of nature, could control them. In short, Marvell wittily subverts all expectations by appearing to argue for sexual freedom in the name of prudence.

Discussion of this difficult poem cannot rest upon any one reading; its elusiveness reminds us of Marvell's complexity of vision and shows us that his is an art which achieves most of its effect by subtle implications and which examines profound abstractions through the immediate or tangible. In some ways the pessimistic and destructive conclusion of 'To His Coy Mistress' recalls the complex contraries of contemplation and activity involved in the 'Horatian Ode': that in the affairs of life to be passive is to surrender responsibility over time and destiny; while, on the other hand, to be active, 'to make time run', asserts responsibility, but its consequences may contradict the original intention.

Pastoral experiments

In the pastoral genre Marvell demonstrates his talent for giving freshness and originality to an ancient and well-established poetic tradition. Where the Spenserians had presented Arcadian idylls and elaborate allegories, in the 1650s Marvell engaged less certain and more complex realities. Marvell's use of nature in these poems is complex, and diverse influences can be noted. Apart from the classical pastorals initiated by Theocritus (*c*.300–*c*.260BC), first and foremost was the Christian tradition's nostalgia for Eden, the earthly paradise. Then there was French *Jouissance* ('enjoyment') poetry, emulated by such Caroline poets as Lovelace and Randolph, which took the conventions of the pastoral and transformed it into a cultivated libertinism which exalted sensuality as a consequence of innocence. Another influence more congenial to Marvell was Montaigne, for whom the garden was a place for contemplation where the senses were controlled by reason.

In *Lycidas* Milton had demonstrated that both the conventions of the pastoral and its Christian symbolism could be turned to contemporary comment. In the 'Mower' poems Marvell marks a radical departure from these conventions by his substitution of a Mower for the shepherd, and an opposition between man-made gardens and the wild meadows of nature. Take, for example, these lines from 'The Mower Against Gardens':

> Luxurious Man, to bring his Vice in use,
>   Did after him the World seduce:
> And from the fields the Flow'rs and Plants allure,
>   Where Nature was most plain and pure.

In an ironic juxtaposition of associations the Mower, advocate of nature and disclaimer of man-made gardens, is an emblem of alienated man. Amidst the meadows his seasonal cutting makes him an emblem for death and time, and subject to the irony that while he opposes the cultivated gardens for their reversals of the natural order, he himself destroys the 'wild and fragrant Innocence' of the open fields.

'The Mower's Song' is a playful love lament within pastoral conventions, but under Marvell's hands it also becomes a powerful image of man's alienation within the natural world—'My Mind was once the true survey/ Of all these medows fresh and gay'—and of man's capacity to destroy. What the Mower experiences at the hands of his unkind mistress is what he also wreaks upon the natural world:

> But what you in Compassion ought,
> Shall now by my Revenge be wrought:
> And Flow'rs, and Grass, and I and all,
> Will in one common Ruine fall.
>   For *Juliana* comes, and She
> What I do to the Grass, does to my Thoughts and Me.

In short, the harmonious relationship between Man and Nature which is at the heart of the pastoral genre, does not exist for Marvell. Within the natural order if man acts at all, it is as a destroyer.

The questions Marvell raises in these poems are also presented at some length in 'Upon Appleton House, to My Lord Fairfax' where Marvell combines the natural world and man-made gardens, and makes of Appleton House a type of Eden. Long and complex, the poem can serve as a virtual thesaurus for themes and issues raised in his other works. Praise of a patron's estate was a commonplace in poems advocating the advantages of rural life. Marvell traces the history of the house with humour (particularly its former use as a convent); he contrasts its orderly agriculture with the chaos of the Civil War, and the retired life of its owner with worldly ambitions; and he praises its occupants, especially Mary Fairfax. The terms of Marvell's argument anticipate the claims made on behalf of Cromwell in the 'Horatian Ode'. Fairfax's own qualities present him as the rightful inheritor of the estate, while his disposition of it, which demonstrates his capacity to order it in harmony with nature, reflects his moral qualities:

> But all things are composed here
> Like Nature, orderly and near . . . (IV.25–6).

Symbolically the estate is both an Eden and a Noah's ark, an emblem of paradise and salvation in a society wracked by contradictions. As such the sense of a Fall—whether that of Original Sin or Civil War—is not forgotten. The pun implicit in *Nun Apple*ton (no apple), which reminds us of the original disobedience of Adam and Eve, is captured in these lines:

> Oh Thou, that dear and happy Isle
> The Garden of the World ere while,
> Thou *Paradise* of four Seas,
> Which *Heaven* planted us to please,
> But, to exclude the World, did guard
> With watry if not flaming Sword;
> What luckless Apple did we tast,
> To make us Mortal, and The Wast? (XLI.321 – 8)

Here even rotting oaks enforce the Edenic symbolism, with their reminder of human frailty, but their fall is retained within a pattern ordered by a kindly divine providence: 'the Oake seems to fall content,/ Viewing the Treason's Punishment.'

Here too the issue of the meditative and the active life recurs though it is not developed. In the woods the poet is an *'easie Philosopher'* in *'Natures mystick Book.'* The attractions of the contemplative life are clearly felt but Marvell wittily concedes that its charms may not entirely suit him:

> But, lest your Fetters prove too weak,
> Ere I your Silken Bondage break,
> Do you, *O Brambles*, chain me too,
> And courteous *Briars* nail me through. (LXXVII.613–16)

Political poetry

> The forward Youth that would appear
> Must now forsake his *Muses* dear,
> Nor in the Shadows sing
> His Numbers languishing. ('An Horatian Ode', lines 1–4)

Where Fairfax's life had moved from involvement to retirement, Marvell's thought moved steadily from rural reflections towards political involvement. Of Marvell's works, few poems provoke a more mixed response, more debate and admiration tinged with suspicion than those poems with a clearly political subject. 'An Horatian Ode upon Cromwel's Return from Ireland' challenges the reader by its vexatious discrepancies between tone and subject, its mixture of Horatian understatement and the extravagance associated with the style of the Latin poet Lucan (AD39–65). While the style suggests objectivity, its ambivalent and paradoxical expression of admiration leave it open to differing interpretations as either satiric or sincere.

These ambiguities precisely mirror the complexity of cause and effect, motive and error. While, on the one hand, Cromwell is shown to be a man of the times, thrown up by the necessity of events, in the context of which traditional concepts—'antient Rights'—no longer apply; yet, on the other hand, he is ambiguous as a hero, and his 'reserved and austere' public demeanour seems less convincing in the light of the 'wiser Art' which connived at Charles I's escape and execution. The complex juxtapositions continue to qualify the movements of thought. The King appears a 'Royal Actor', that is one who is gracious but ineffectual when compared to Cromwell, who is the man 'that does both act and know'. At this point the poem recalls, most explicitly, Marvell's preoccupation with the rival states of action and contemplation, and moves closest to sincere praise.

Yet even then the final word is ambiguous. Marvell's view of history links cause and effect and leaves the reader with the ominous couplet 'The same *Arts* that did *gain*/ A *Pow'r* must it *maintain*.' The earlier couplet which registers the height of Cromwell's powers 'Nor yet grown stiffer with Command,/ But still in the *Republick's* hand:' deceives by its innocuous monosyllables. But when the regular iambic rhythm is heard, the stresses fall upon the second word in each line, 'yet' and 'still', and suggest that Cromwell's actions may yet contradict the intentions of those who installed him.

The variety of Marvell's political poetry is most impressive. The earlier poems provide evidence of his initial royalist sympathies—for example, the poems on Lovelace and Hastings. 'Tom May's Death' is usually dated after the 'Horatian Ode' and perplexes critics by its lack of the subtlety—poetical and political—of the Ode; it is a direct attack upon May for his switch of allegiance from King to Parliament. 'The First Anniversary of the Government under O.C.' is the most obvious of Marvell's political poems: this is a panegyrical defence of the dissolution of the 'Barebones' Parliament and the establishment of the Protectorate, and was written after Marvell had come under the personal influence of Milton and Cromwell. Through his use of sustained similes and biblical and classical analogies, the events described appear elevated, and this effect is further developed by the energetic lines which suggest heroic movement. Closely reasoned, urbane and yet compressed, the poem anticipates the evolution of Augustan clarity from Metaphysical poetry.

Marvell as a religious poet

As a religious poet Marvell contrasts directly with the other Meta-physical poets. Where they use the personal lyric, Marvell generally favours the dialogue poem. The form is central to his interests: where Donne engages his urgent sense of guilt, Herbert the possibility of futility and the desirability of resignation, and Vaughan and Traherne move towards a mystical vision, Marvell's concerns weigh the tensions between pleasure and duty, idleness and activity, soul and body. Nearly all address the tension between nature and grace and its related anti-theses, and move towards some sort of resolution. At the risk of over-simplification, the conflict is essentially a Puritan one, the distinction between what is social rather than personal, practical rather than moral.

A difficulty with Marvell's religious poems is that, though few in number, they cover a wide range of poetic approaches and forms—emblems, debate, meditation, pastoral eclogue and a hymn of praise—and yet fail to utilise the self-conscious speaker who dominates most other seventeeth-century religious verse.

Some religious dialogues are cast in the pastoral mould. 'A Dialogue Between Thyrsis and Dorinda' and 'Clorinda and Damon' are good examples. The latter in particular with its conversion of pagan sensual-ity by Christian virtue suggests Marvell's moral earnestness. Others, however—for not all of them are dialogues—are remarkable achieve-ments, in particular 'A Dialogue Between the Resolved Soul and Creat-ed Pleasure', 'On A Drop of Dew', 'The Coronet', the emblem poem 'Eyes and Tears' which demands comparison with Crashaw's 'The Weeper', and the intensely lyrical 'Bermudas' where Marvell's vivid imagery echoes the sensuousness of 'The Garden'. Marvell associated the islands of Bermuda with the Puritan exiles he had known flee there, while he also drew upon the island's association in popular imagination with being a type of earthly paradise, as in Shakespeare's *The Tempest* (printed 1623). A few lines may show how the poem is a telling instance of Marvell's fusion of the exotic and sensuous with the religious.

He hangs in the shades the Orange bright,
Like golden Lamps in a green Night.
And does in the Pomgranates close,
Jewels more rich than *Ormus* shows.
He makes the Figs our mouths to meet;
And throws the Melons at our feet.
But Apples plants of such a price,
No Tree could ever bear them twice . . .
   Thus sang they, in the *English* boat,
An holy and a chearful Note,

And all the way, to guide their Chime,
With falling Oars they kept the time.

'The Coronet' is in the sub-genre of a wreath or crown of praise poem—something offered to God. This was an image that figured in the various emblem books of the period, and it is taken up in Donne's *La Corona* and Herbert's 'A Wreath'. Marvell begins his poem with a proposal to link the orders of grace and nature by poetic art, then acknowledges the folly of this, and closes with a humility which confesses that the transformation he seeks is dependent upon life and poetry being destroyed—so that Grace may act. In this sense the poem demonstrates Marvell's rather Puritan aesthetics and the dichotomies which pervade most of these poems.

Standing apart from these is 'The Garden' with that most typical theme of Marvell's, the choice between contemplation or action. Yet in Marvell's case to establish rigid boundaries between poetic kinds is to falsify the rich sense of complexity his poetry offers and to forget that the ancient debate between the virtues of action and contemplation was mainly religious.

Appreciation of the religious nature of the poem must not be at the expense of an awareness of its magnificent language. Puritan though Marvell was in his sympathies, 'The Garden' is a shining example of his ability to generate luscious images that are remarkable for their unqualified sensuality. In vivid and evocative language he charges our senses with an almost tactile appreciation of the imagined scene. The fifth, sixth and seventh stanzas amply show his ability to command a rich and sensuous diction:

What wond'rous Life is this I lead!
Ripe Apples drop about my head;
The Luscious Clusters of the Vine
Upon my Mouth do crush their Wine;
The Nectarine, and curious Peach,
Into my hands themselves do reach;
Stumbling on Melons, as I pass,
Insnar'd with Flow'rs, I fall on Grass.

Mean while the Mind, from pleasure less,
Withdraws into its happiness:
The Mind, that Ocean where each kind
Does streight its own resemblance find;
Yet it creates, transcending these,
Far other Worlds, and other Seas;
Annihilating all that's made
To a green Thought in a green Shade.

> Here at the Fountains sliding foot,
> Or at some Fruit-trees mossy root,
> Casting the Bodies Vest aside,
> My Soul into the boughs does glide:
> There like a Bird it sits, and sings,
> Then whets, and combs its silver Wings;
> And, till prepar'd for longer flight,
> Waves in its Plumes the various Light.

The poem begins with withdrawal from the world, ambition and love—signified by the emblems of 'the Palm, the Oke, or Bayes'. In the garden's Edenic setting, activity being replaced by stillness, the poet is able to experience a new relationship with nature. Stanza V marks a momentary sense of Edenic innocence which he expresses with urbane wit: 'Stumbling on Melons, as I pass, / Insnar'd with Flow'rs, I fall on Grass.' The theological wit of this is strengthened if we remember that the Greek for 'apple' is 'Melon' and 'Grass' would have been pronounced 'grace'. In this situation Marvell discerns a concord between nature and grace rather than an opposition, and contemplates the divine through the natural.

The movement of the poem is inwards, through the garden into the mind. 'Annihilation' is a term associated with mystical prayer, and, even if this is not strictly appropriate, the sense is clear: the poet experiences a transformed vision of the world, 'a green Thought in a green Shade.' This movement culminates in a conventional image of the soul as a bird 'prepar'd for longer flight' which may denote both mystical ecstasy and an anticipation of death.

Characteristically Marvell provides another movement to the poem, and demonstrates, as did Donne, that it is possible to write a religious poem that is also humorous. The final two stanzas reinstate the urbane and witty tone, touch upon various conventions such as the idea that Eden would have been perfect without Eve, and return the poet and reader to the world. Yet even here the poem is tightly wrought. Earlier in the poem the colours 'red and white', the emblems of female love and associated with libertine garden poetry, were supplanted by the green of Edenic innocence and contemplation. Here, as a resumé, Marvell demonstrates that the love women offer is the wrong love. The path to be pursued in the contemplative life is that of divine love, and nature is shown to be the means whereby that may be understood and achieved.

CHRONOLOGICAL TABLE

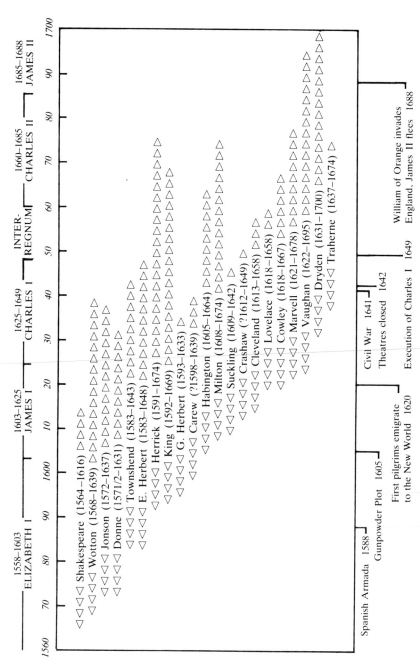

Suggestions for further reading

ALVAREZ, A: *The School of Donne*, Chatto & Windus, London, 1970.
BROWNE, THOMAS: *Religio Medici and other works*, ed. L.C. Martin, Oxford University Press, Oxford, 1964.
BUSH, D: *English Literature in the Earlier Seventeenth Century 1600–1660*, Oxford University Press, Oxford, rev. edn, 1962.
FORD, B (ED.): *A Guide to English Literature*, Vol. 3 *From Donne to Marvell*, Penguin, Harmondsworth, rev. edn, 1962.
LEISHMANN, J.B: *The Metaphysical Poets: Donne, Herbert, Vaughan, Traherne*, Oxford University Press, Oxford, 1934.
LEWIS, C.S: *The Discarded Image: An Introduction to Medieval and Renaissance Literature*, Cambridge University Press, Cambridge, 1964.
MARTZ, L.L: *The Poetry of Meditation: A Study in English Religious Literature of the Seventeenth Century*, Yale University Press, New Haven, Connecticut, 1955.
RIVERS.I: *Classical and Christian Ideas in English Renaissance Poetry*, George Allen & Unwin, London, 1979.
TUVE, R: *Elizabethan and Metaphysical Imagery*, University of Chicago Press, Chicago, 1947.
WALTON, I: *The Lives of Dr John Donne, Sir Henry Wotton, Mr Richard Hooker, Mr George Herbert*, ed. G. Saintsbury, Oxford University Press, Oxford, 1927.
WIND, E: *Pagan Mysteries in the Renaissance*, Peregrine, Harmondsworth, 1967.

Index

York Handbooks: list of titles

YORK HANDBOOKS form a companion series to York Notes and are designed to meet the wider needs of students of English and related fields. Each volume is a compact study of a given subject area, written by an authority with experience in communicating the essential ideas to students of all levels.

AN INTRODUCTORY GUIDE TO ENGLISH LITERATURE
by MARTIN STEPHEN

PREPARING FOR EXAMINATIONS IN ENGLISH LITERATURE
by NEIL McEWAN

EFFECTIVE STUDYING
by STEVE ROBERTSON *and* DAVID SMITH

THE ENGLISH NOVEL
by IAN MILLIGAN

ENGLISH POETRY
by CLIVE T PROBYN

DRAMA: PLAYS, THEATRE AND PERFORMANCE
by MARGERY MORGAN

AN INTRODUCTION TO LINGUISTICS
by LORETO TODD

STUDYING CHAUCER
by ELISABETH BREWER

STUDYING SHAKESPEARE
by MARTIN STEPHEN *and* PHILIP FRANKS

AN A·B·C OF SHAKESPEARE
by P. C. BAYLEY

STUDYING MILTON
by GEOFFREY M. RIDDEN

STUDYING CHARLES DICKENS
by K. J. FIELDING

STUDYING THOMAS HARDY
by LANCE ST JOHN BUTLER

STUDYING THE BRONTËS
by SHEILA SULLIVAN

STUDYING JAMES JOYCE
by HARRY BLAMIRES

ENGLISH LITERATURE FROM THE THIRD WORLD
by TREVOR JAMES

ENGLISH USAGE
by COLIN G. HEY

ENGLISH GRAMMAR
by LORETO TODD

STYLE IN ENGLISH PROSE
by NEIL McEWAN

AN INTRODUCTION TO LITERARY CRITICISM
by RICHARD DUTTON

A DICTIONARY OF LITERARY TERMS
by MARTIN GRAY

READING THE SCREEN
An Introduction to Film Studies
by JOHN IZOD

The author of this Handbook

TREVOR JAMES was educated at Victoria University, New Zealand, and King's College, London. An Anglican priest, he has taught English at Waikato University, New Zealand, and is now a Senior Lecturer in English at the Darwin Institute of Technology where he lectures in Commonwealth literature. A Research Associate of Flinders University Centre for Research in the New English Literatures, and a Visiting Fellow of the Australian National University, he has written extensively on various aspects of Commonwealth literature and is the author of the York Handbook *English Literature from the Third World*.